ENCOURAGING
PHYSICAL DEVELOPMENT
through MOVEMENT-PLAY

D0086224

SAGE | 50 YEARS

SAGE was founded in 1965 by Sara Miller McCune to support the dissemination of usable knowledge by publishing innovative and high-quality research and teaching content. Today, we publish more than 750 journals, including those of more than 300 learned societies, more than 800 new books per year, and a growing range of library products including archives, data, case studies, reports, conference highlights, and video. SAGE remains majority-owned by our founder, and after Sara's lifetime will become owned by a charitable trust that secures our continued independence.

Los Angeles | London | Washington DC | New Delhi | Singapore | Boston

Miami-Dade College
Homestead Campus Library

500 College Terrace
Homestead, FL 33030-6009

ENCOURAGING
PHYSICAL DEVELOPMENT
through MOVEMENT-PLAY

CAROL ARCHER
AND IRAM SIRAJ

⑨SAGE

Los Angeles | London | New Delhi
Singapore | Washington DC | Boston

Los Angeles | London | New Delhi
Singapore | Washington DC | Boston

SAGE Publications Ltd
1 Oliver's Yard
55 City Road
London EC1Y 1SP

SAGE Publications Inc.
2455 Teller Road
Thousand Oaks, California 91320

SAGE Publications India Pvt Ltd
B 1/I 1 Mohan Cooperative Industrial Area
Mathura Road
New Delhi 110 044

SAGE Publications Asia-Pacific Pte Ltd
3 Church Street
#10-04 Samsung Hub
Singapore 049483

Editor: Amy Jarrold
Editorial assistant: George Knowles
Production editor: Tom Bedford
Copyeditor: Michelle Clark
Proofreader: Audrey Scriven
Indexer: Cathy Heath
Marketing manager: Dilhara Attygalle
Cover design: Wendy Scott
Typeset by: C&M Digitals (P) Ltd, Chennai, India
Printed by CPI Group (UK) Ltd, Croydon, CR0 4YY

© Carol Archer and Iram Siraj, 2015

First published 2015

Apart from any fair dealing for the purposes of research or private study, or criticism or review, as permitted under the Copyright, Designs and Patents Act, 1988, this publication may be reproduced, stored or transmitted in any form, or by any means, only with the prior permission in writing of the publishers, or in the case of reprographic reproduction, in accordance with the terms of licences issued by the Copyright Licensing Agency. Enquiries concerning reproduction outside those terms should be sent to the publishers.

Library of Congress Control Number: 2014953071

British Library Cataloguing in Publication data

A catalogue record for this book is available from the British Library

MIX
Paper from responsible sources
FSC
www.fsc.org   FSC® C013604

ISBN 978-1-4462-9711-7
ISBN 978-1-4462-9712-4 (pbk)

At SAGE we take sustainability seriously. Most of our products are printed in the UK using FSC papers and boards. When we print overseas we ensure sustainable papers are used as measured by the Egmont grading system. We undertake an annual audit to monitor our sustainability.

Contents

Figures and tables

Figures

Tables

About the authors

Carol Archer has taught in early childhood education and primary schools for over two decades and is currently an advisory teacher for the Integrated Early Years Service in the London borough of Camden. She also works as a movement-play practitioner/consultant for other education authorities. She finished her Master's degree in early years education at the Institute of Education, University of London, in 2011, and recently published a paper with Iram Siraj on 'Measuring the quality of movement-play in early childhood education settings' in the *European Early Childhood Education Research Journal*. She is passionate about promoting physical development through movement-play for all young children from birth to six years of age in this under-researched, under-theorised and under-practised area of learning.

Iram Siraj is Professor of Early Childhood Education at the UCL Institute of Education, University College London, and the University of Wollongong in Australia. Iram's recent research projects have included leading on the Evaluation of the Foundation Phase across Wales and she is a principal investigator for the major Department for Education's 17-year study, the Effective Pre-school, Primary and Secondary Education (EPPSE 3–16, 1997–2014) project, and the influential Researching Effective Pedagogy in the Early Years (REPEY) project. She has led on longitudinal studies/randomised controlled trials as a principal investigator in a number of countries, including the UK, Australia and Ireland. She is currently a specialist adviser to the House of Commons Select Committee on early education and has undertaken reviews of the Foundation Phase for the Welsh Government and the workforce for the Scottish Government. She has also published widely.

Acknowledgements

First and foremost our thanks go to the children and practitioners who have contributed so much to our understanding of young children's movement development, and the many children and parents who gave permission to use photographs to illustrate the movement patterns and physical activities printed in this book.

Special thanks go to all the children and staff at Agar Children's Centre, Collingham Gardens Nursery and 1a Children's Centre for all their time, patience, invaluable help and contributions. In particular, Teresa Barker, Mikelia Fugolin, Katharine Jerrom and Marilyn Sherwood-Clinton for their unceasing support, enthusiasm and sense of humour during the whole process. Thanks also go to Carole Limtouch and Monica Piszczyk for their valuable work with parents and their contributions.

Many thanks to Lynn Linsell, senior manager at Camden Integrated Early Years Service, for her advice and contribution to the template included in Chapter 6 on policy, and to Regents Park Children's Centre for their current Physical Development policy.

Thanks also go to Camilla Saunders and Helen Simpson who read and made constructive and helpful comments on early drafts.

This work on movement-play began with training from Jasmin Pasch, to whom we owe many thanks for her ongoing support, and countless discussions with Carol. Thanks also go to Bette Lamont, who has been a constant inspiration, to Jacqui Cousins for providing direction and support in the early stages of this work, and to Susan Hill who encouraged the development of the assessment scale for movement-play which Camden Early Years Advisors contributed to.

1
Movement-play and its influence on young children's development

What is movement-play?

Movement-play is about children moving in specific ways as they go through a developmental sequence of significant movement patterns that link the body and brain. Early reflexes, senses and movement are the young child's route to learning, which is through the body. Movement and sensory experiences are crucial for the child's social and emotional development, behaviour and learning. Movement stimulates the neurological system that fires and wires the brain, forming a multitude of connections that lay important foundations for the young child's future learning and development. In this way, movement-play is more than physical activity but does not preclude it.

This chapter explores neuroscience and neurological dysfunction in relation to children's movement and physical development. This will be important to the reader as background information in relation to the more practical chapters coming later in the book.

Physical activity and health

Research has exposed the link between exercise and health benefits since the 1950s (Tremarche et al., 2007), but it was only near the end of the last century that it began to be taken seriously (van Praag, 2009). Today, it is common knowledge that physical activity can mitigate the risk of heart disease, type 2 diabetes, osteoporosis, hypertension, cardiovascular disease (DH, 2011) and depression (van Praag, 2009) and improve cognition

(Cotman et al., 2007; van Praag, 2009). Evidence now shows that promoting physical activity across the lifespan can reverse trends in obesity and disease (DH, 2011) and improve brain health, resilience, learning and memory (Cotman and Berchtold, 2007; van Praag, 2009).

Recent lifestyle changes have, however, resulted in increasing amounts of inactivity among even the youngest children and young adults. The use of computers, Internet surfing, video game playing and television have led to ever-increasing numbers becoming overweight or obese (DH, 2011). As a consequence, the last ten years have seen a rising number of young people with health problems that are more usually associated with adults. Mounting concern about the state of health of the youngest children has meant the need for more movement activity has never been greater.

Linking movement with five areas of early childhood development

How does movement and physical development fit in with all the areas of early childhood development? The five broad areas of children's learning and development are:

- physical
- communication and language
- self-regulation
- cognitive
- social and emotional development.

These cover every aspect of a young child's life. Although each area is addressed separately, children's development is interconnected and therefore occurs across all areas.

Physical development

Physical development includes the child's ability to gradually control movement, coordination, balance, fine and gross motor skills. By repeating specific movement patterns, infants eventually learn to balance away from the floor and crawl on all fours. When infants learn to crawl, they put pressure on their hands and fingers through their arms and shoulders. This is how they begin to develop the fine motor skills essential for writing, drawing, throwing and catching a ball, building with blocks and using scissors.

Over time, infants pull themselves up onto their feet, walking and balancing with skill. Later, more challenging and vigorous movement activities are learned and refined, such as climbing high on a climbing frame or wall, hanging upside down, or swinging high on a swing or accomplishing somersaults.

Core concepts of maths are embedded in the body through a sense of rhythm, patterns, sequencing and space. To understand spatial relationships, children must first learn about their own body position and size, which can be done effectively through movement. Movement is at the heart of young children's physical development and is inextricably linked to other areas of learning.

Communication and language

Body language is a fundamental part of communication for very young children and will come before the development of spoken language. When children have developed their movement vocabulary, they will be able to understand the body language of others. Early forms of communication, suggests Maude (2010), are non-verbal as babies successfully use gestures and body language as a means of conveying messages between themselves and their carers and vice versa. Movement conversations can be sustained as the infant and adult make eye contact, touch, smile, change facial gestures and move their bodies in response to each other.

Some people feel more comfortable communicating through body language. Speaking on BBC Radio 4, Akram Khan, a famous contemporary dancer, said he was so shy when he was young that he didn't talk much to other children, especially girls. Then he won a disco competition in his teens and discovered that his body was his language. 'Once I discovered dance,' he said, 'I knew that this is my language. My dance has never failed me. It is my companion.' Akram Khan developed verbal means of communication more easily once he developed his movement vocabulary. Similarly, adults can provide babies and young children with the language and companionship of movement and dance. It is possible to develop a deep bonding experience through moving together with another person.

Maude (2010: 1) reminds us that, 'language acquisition through moving cannot be underestimated'. The acquisition of body language associated with movement includes nouns, such as the names for body parts; verbs, as children lie down, sit on a chair, stand or point; adverbs, such as slowly, quickly; and prepositions, such as up, down, behind, over, under.

Physical literacy can be developed by translating movements into spoken language in a variety of contexts by using descriptive, directional and action words that young children can experience and then use themselves.

Self-regulation

Young children accused of fidgeting are not likely to respond to an adult's demands to sit still. Instead, these children just need to move! Young children learn by actively engaging with and participating in the learning process and, therefore, the classroom environment needs to support the child's body in order that the mind can develop and learn. Many benefits flow from the child actively moving because they learn through their body first and foremost.

Children learn to translate what they physically experience into information they can use to regulate their thoughts, emotions and behaviour (Blair and Diamond, 2008). Infants begin to translate soothing touch and the sound of soft voices into signals that help them to develop self-calming skills. Young children begin to freely move their bodies and gradually begin to learn to inhibit urges to grab things for themselves, then how to wait for their turn, which helps them regulate emotional tension.

When young children learn through their bodies, they are also developing their minds as the two work in partnership together. Children in classrooms that honour their innate need to move learn to regulate their emotions and intellectual development by being provided with numerous and varied opportunities for their bodies to do what they need to.

Cognitive development

Cognitive development occurs rapidly during the preschool years. Neuroscientists have found in their experiments that learning in terms of cognition, memory and behaviour occurs through physical activity. Goddard Blythe (2005a) suggests that physical skills, including balance, posture and coordination, need to be secured in the early years in order for children to enter the school system better equipped to cope with the demands of the classroom. When specific movement activities, such as tummy time, crawling, rolling, swinging, hanging upside down and somersaults, are repeated, areas of the brain are stimulated. It is through repeating specific movement patterns that young children develop their ability to sit still, concentrate, coordinate their hands and eyes when writing and control their eye movements for reading, thus influencing their later academic achievement.

Social and emotional development

Understanding how to communicate, share, make friends and get along with others in the first six years is carried out with more ease through physical activity. Through movement activities or games, children learn rules of behaviour, they learn to read the facial expressions of others and express their own emotions, such as fear, sadness, anger and happiness. As a baby is raised high in the air by a trusted adult she squeals with delight. The first time a young child attempts to hang upside down on a climbing frame he may feel fearful until an observant adult comes to his side or holds him in a gentle, reassuring way. Healthy play experiences such as everyday rough and tumble activities promote social bonds, and nourish social learning and the development of emotionally healthy minds (Panksepp, 2010). When children and parents rough and tumble together, it is a chance to strengthen the bond between them. Sharing stillness and silence with a peer or adult can impact on the children's well-being and feelings of connectedness.

All these areas of child development are not separate entities: physical development, communication, social and emotional and cognitive development and self-regulation do not mature separately from one another. There is an overlap and interconnectedness between them. When children learn something related to one area, it impacts on the others. Children do not differentiate between thinking, feeling and moving because the mind and body are inextricably linked.

Neuroscience research, the brain, exercise and learning and their application to education

We will now turn to neuroscience and how advances in research have informed us about how the brain functions. These findings have considerable implications for early education in terms of teaching and learning, and none more so than those concerning children's earliest years.

The child's body is inextricably linked to the brain, which develops and restructures itself based on experiences. The brain receives information from the senses and integrates it, and the body takes action quickly and efficiently precisely because of the insulation called myelin that forms around the axons. This speeds up communication between neurons.

Myelination begins when the foetus is in the womb, continues throughout childhood and adolescence (Rutter et al., 2010) and relates closely to developmental milestones (Goddard Blythe, 2005a). The child's experiences help to fine-tune the brain's responses to the stimulation it receives. This beneficial process does, however, also highlight the vulnerability of young children's brains, as they can, as a result, be susceptible to developmental problems if their environment is impoverished and experience of movement patterns is limited.

Such knowledge about the brain is relatively new – much is still being discovered and not all is yet fully understood. The use of functional magnetic resonance imaging (fMRI) over the last twenty-five years or so has allowed scientists to see images inside the human brain. These show areas where, as a result of neural activity, oxygen-rich blood is flowing to those active regions of the brain. Blood flowing in specific areas of the brain suggests that particular functions have been activated. For example, a language task will activate several different regions of the brain as there is not just one area that is responsible for that function: several areas can contribute (Greenfield, 2001).

Functional magnetic resonance imaging (fMRI) is a non-invasive procedure widely used in brain science and neuroscientists are presently seeking to explore if they can more accurately map the human brain's 'wiring system' through directly measuring neural activity. Despite its relative newness fMRI has certainly begun to open up our understanding of how the brain works and further research is progressing and developing relatively quickly, 'but the adventure is only really just beginning' (Greenfield, 2001: 192).

The brain is an extremely complex, fascinating, constantly active, living organ. Everyone has a unique brain, developing in response to a person's genetic make-up and the influence of the environment, both of which affect learning ability (The Royal Society (TRS), 2011). Environmental and genetic influences begin while in the womb. After birth, genetic make-up interacts with environmental factors, such as diet, toxins and social interactions (TRS, 2011: 3). Children's experiences, particularly those that stimulate the brain in their earliest years, have a profound effect on structuring their brains (Goddard Blythe, 2005b; Hannaford, 1995; Lamont, 2007b; Macintyre and McVitty, 2004). Further considerations are the effects of early deprivation and poverty, as these interact with a genetic predisposition, affecting future mental health problems and, as a consequence, influence learning (TRS, 2011). This is important information for those interested in children and learning as it is education that can affect young children's well-being and has future economic benefits for the individual and society (TRS, 2011).

Neuroscience research continues to help us understand how the brain functions and is revealing approaches to teaching and learning. Neuroresearch in education, however, is still relatively new and we are advised to be cautious in its application (Bruer, 2002; Jensen, 2005; TRS, 2011). Nonetheless, the findings from brain-based learning influence many aspects of education, such as teaching strategies, special education, learning environments and assessments, to name just a few (Jensen, 2005). Schoolchildren in England typically spend 190 days each year at school for 12 years, accumulating over 12,000 hours of time during their school lives with teachers.

Increasing numbers of infants and young children are attending early education settings, including early childhood settings and school settings (DfE, 2012). As children's brains are susceptible to environmental influences, changes in the brain will undoubtedly take place as a result of their experiences at preschool/school. It would appear, therefore, that preschool/school is the optimum place to influence learning (TRS, 2011).

For some time now, neuroscientists experimenting on animals (Cotman et al., 2007; Hillman et al., 2008; O'Callaghan et al., 2007; O'Callaghan et al., 2009; van Praag, 2009) have shed light on the developing brain and learning, with insights that help us to understand teaching and learning in new ways (TRS, 2011). For example, neuroscientists have demonstrated the benefits of exercise on brain function. Research on animals has revealed that exercise increases the number of new neurons in the hippocampus, an area of the brain that is important for learning, memory and cognition (O'Callaghan et al., 2007; van Praag, 2009). Indeed, research has shown that physical activity has a profound effect on memory (van Praag, 2009). The more aerobic the activity, the more chemicals are released in the brain, which is associated with synaptic plasticity and results in changes in the neural architecture of the brain (Hillman et al., 2008; Jensen, 2005; van Praag, 2009). Therefore, the more enriched the environment, the greater the number of neural connections.

The brain is made up of billions of brain cells called neurons, with its development beginning in the womb (TRS, 2011). By the time babies are due to be born, they will have most of their neurones (Greenfield, 2001). Each neuron makes about 10,000 connections with other neurons. Some of the brain cells are genetically determined, though many are shaped by experiences after birth, with environmental influences also determining how the brain begins to be organised. Thus, the brain processes stimuli from the body and from the outside world (Greenfield, 2001). Connections between the brain cells are known as synapses, enabling information to travel from one neuron to another. Neurons connect to each other and are strengthened when they are activated so that 'neurons that fire together wire together' (TRS, 2011: 5).

After birth, babies' heads continue to grow to accommodate an ever-increasing brain so, by the time children are four years old, their brains are four times the size they were when they were born (Greenfield, 2001). Every time we move, think, interact, talk, walk, learn and feel or remember something, our neurons are making connections. Young children stimulate these connections as they encounter new experiences by repeating them over and over again in an attempt to make sense of the world around them. In this way, they design their own nervous systems as they encounter choices and challenges.

The brain can learn, change and develop in response to experiences, but those pathways that are not used will be pruned away. Activity and growth in the brain run concurrently and we are advised to use it as much as we can (Greenfield, 2001: 147). Our brains are amazingly adaptable, creating more neuronal connections in response to the demands of the environment, known as experience-dependent plasticity (TRS, 2011: 5).

The child develops as a unique individual as synapses build into complex networks through ongoing childhood experiences. Thus, the brain of a child in their early years is capable of being moulded by experience because of the processes of myelination, synaptogenesis and neural plasticity (Rutter, 2006a). During this period of life, the brain is much more sensitive to experiences than it is in later years.

Myelin is the fatty cells that insulate the axons of neurons. The process of myelination helps faster communication to take place between axons. Sensory and motor areas of the brain are myelinated around the pre-school period (Tierney and Nelson, 2009), whereas connections in other areas of the brain are strengthened later, with the vestibular system, for example, at between six-and-a-half and eight years of age (Goddard Blythe, 2005a). So, the times at which different regions of the brain are myelinated differ, with the process in some regions not having been completed until adolescence or early adulthood (Tierney and Nelson, 2009: 3). The early years, however, are particularly important for the development of the brain. This is when the foundations vital for language, social and emotional development are formed and these are strongly influenced by experiences during this time (Tierney and Nelson, 2009: 3). In this way, experiences in a child's earliest years will influence the development of the brain's architecture. While the brain is constantly changing and developing throughout our lifetimes, it is the early years that lay the foundations for the development of the higher-level functions of the brain.

There are times during childhood and young adulthood when changes in the brain involve more exuberant activity than usual, often called 'sensitive periods' (TRS, 2011: 5). A sensitive period is likely to occur at times of high synaptic density during childhood and extending into young adulthood. These periods have been linked with critical times for learning. Sensitive periods have been identified for certain sensory stimuli, such as vision, speech sounds and emotion, as well as motor and cognitive experiences, such as language. The capacity to learn something specific can be lost or diminished because of limited or no experience of it during a critical period (TRS, 2011). For example, infants' brains are tuned in to the sounds of nearly all languages, but a child will learn the language sounds that they are exposed to most and experience with people close to them (Tierney and Nelson, 2009: 3). Learning a second language later in life is more difficult than it is in early childhood. Indeed, the prime time for learning to read, write and speak a second language is in the child's earliest years and up to about the age of 12, when ears and brains are able to adapt to hear differences in sounds so the child can then articulate them (TRS, 2011). After this time, another language becomes increasingly difficult to learn for most people, if not impossible for some, though not all. Pruning of the synapses is mostly related to experience, so neural pathways that are not used will be eliminated, while those that are activated are strengthened (Tierney and Nelson, 2009). The young child's brain is more sensitive to experiences than later in life and is remarkably adaptable and responsive due to its plasticity.

When it comes to applying this knowledge about sensitive periods for learning to the field of education, there is some contention among neuroscientists (Blakemore and Frith, 2005; Bruer, 2002; Goswami, 2006; Howard-Jones, 2007).

Bruer (2002), linking neuroscience, psychology and education in the study of human cognition, questions claims made about the connection between peak synaptic densities and critical times for learning. He (2002: 1032) is sceptical that neuroscience research has much to offer teachers right now as there is more we need to know about changes in synaptic density and how this process influences mental development and cognition before it should be applied to education. He suggests that, as research progresses, which may take many years, it will undoubtedly contribute to the application of science to education. Until then, Bruer argues, its application to education has 'little practical value' and he advocates that more years of research are carried out for this 'approach to bear fruit'.

Bruer made these claims over a decade ago, although concern among neuroscientists more recently is focused on the 'inappropriate exploitation of neuroscience' (TRS, 2011: 17), as the enthusiasm for neuroscience in education has led to some confusion. For example, neuromyths (Goswami, 2006; Howard-Jones, 2007; TRS, 2011) appear to be dominating ideas about teaching and learning, which, Goswami emphatically argues, need to be eliminated. Neuromyths such as identifying children as either left-brained or right-brained learners are regarded as an 'over literal interpretation of hemispheric specialisation' by Goswami (2006: 2), who also questions labelling children as either visual, auditory or kinaesthetic learners, as well as being sceptical about claims made regarding whole brain learning through a commercial Brain Gym® package. These neuromyths are being adopted as facts when, some argue, they should be regarded as a 'misapplication of science to education' (Goswami, 2006: 2).

It is difficult for educationalists to sift through the volume of information, games, and ideas claiming to be based on neuroscientific evidence in order to identify what is 'independent, accurate and authoritative' (TRS, 2011: 18). If educational neuroscience is to be effective and impact on the quality of learning positively, then a long-term dialogue (TRS, 2011) and interdisciplinary cooperation between educators, policymakers and neuroscientists need to take place to ensure 'scientific validity and educational relevance' (Howard-Jones, 2007: 8).

From this we can see that there appears to be a lack of consensus about the application of brain science in education. Neuroscience, however, has certainly entered into the arena of education and, consequently, it is important that it develops into an effective discipline (TRS, 2011).

Blakemore and Frith (2005: 459) stress the importance of anchoring education in neuroscientific evidence-based research, highlighting that, 'now is the time to explore the implications of brain science for education'. Research on the brain and learning 'could influence the way we think about teaching', which may 'transform educational strategies and enable us to design educational programmes that optimise learning' (Blakemore and Frith, 2005: 460). Indeed, The Royal Society (2011: 19) of scientists suggests that neuroscience be considered as a tool for 'science-based education policy' to 'help assess the performance and impact' of a variety of educational approaches. The Society also recommends that neuroscience be included in initial teacher education courses and as part of continued professional development to ensure that 'research is critically discussed, evaluated and effectively applied' (TRS, 2011: 21). Clearly, more communication is needed between neuroscientists, cognitive psychologists and educationalists in order that necessary steps can be taken to implement the most credible research into learning environments for children from birth to 6 years of age.

Movement patterns, development and learning

A significant contribution has been made to our knowledge about the influence of movement on a child's neurological system, learning and development by a number of practitioners and researchers (Goddard Blythe, 2005a; Hannaford, 1995; Jensen, 2005; Lamont, 2007a; Macintyre and McVitty, 2004; McPhillips and Sheehy, 2004). Working in the field of neurological reorganisation and dysfunction, they have first-hand experience of investigating the relationship between movement activity, development and learning with regard to children from birth through primary school and beyond. Persuaded by the influence that early movement patterns have on the neurological system and learning, they are convinced of the importance of its application in early movement-play education.

For example, in her work as a developmental movement therapist, Lamont (2007b) has found that when infants repeat specific movement patterns, such as tummy crawling and crawling on all fours, important developments take place and particular areas of the brain are stimulated. Conversely, when babies miss out on significant movements, then critical functions are compromised, affecting later development and, thus, their ability to reach their full potential at school (Lamont, 2007c). Goddard Blythe (2005a) has developed a programme of physical exercises based on reflexes and movements that infants normally make in the first year of life and has evidence to show the enhanced literacy skills of children who have participated in these exercises at school.

Several weeks after conception, the growing foetus will move in the womb, increasing activity at a later stage by twisting, stretching and kicking. The first year after birth is also a critically important time for the young infant, as this is the time that basic movement patterns are developing. This is indeed the best time for infants to develop these early movements. They do not have to be taught as infants, given the space, time and encouragement, will strive to do all that is required of them to move.

Infants need to be free to explore these significant movement patterns and, in this way, they will design and redesign their complex nervous system (Hannaford, 1995: 22). Movement is the basis of everything we do, from walking, getting dressed and brushing our teeth to talking.

Every infant goes through a series of developmental movement stages before the brain and body can operate at their full potential (Lamont, 2007a: 2). These stages can be revisited at any time and introduced to children who missed out on any of these movement patterns in their earliest years. Learning for the infant and young child is grounded in the body and is inseparably linked to reflexes, the senses and movement (Goddard Blythe, 2005a; Hannaford, 1995; Lamont, 2007b; Macintyre and McVitty, 2004; McPhillips et al., 2000).

Reflexes

Work on foetal movements at the Royal Maternity Hospital in Belfast by McPhillips et al. (2000) revealed that primary reflexes assist and enable development of the architecture of the central nervous system. Primary reflexes are therefore playing a critical role during foetal development that helps the foetus kick, move its arms and legs and suck its thumb. Reflexes that begin during life in the womb are critical for the survival of the baby after birth, such as rooting and sucking, which are triggered in the search for food when the baby is hungry (McPhillips et al., 2000). The newborn is full of primary (sometimes called primitive) reflexes, which all play a part in continuing to organise the brain and body during the first year of life.

After birth, the new baby wriggles its legs and arms around in search of a movement pattern. The baby begins to reach and grasp objects in an attempt to bring them to its midline and then to the mouth. These reflexes are actions that direct the baby's movements in early stages of development.

Some reflexes may be familiar to those who have had contact with a baby, such as the Moro reflex, sometimes called the startle reflex, activating the fight or flight response, or the neck reflexes, such as the symmetrical (STNR) and asymmetrical tonic neck reflex (ATNR) or the Palmar reflex. Goddard Blythe (2005a, 2005b) has written extensively about primary reflexes, how they influence the child's development and how, if reflexes persist, this can interfere with the child's future learning. For example, the ATNR normally disappears when a baby is around six months old (Goddard Blythe, 2005a, 2005b; McPhillips et al., 2000), but, if it persists, can indicate developmental delays.

Given the space to lie flat, an infant's face will turn to one side and the arm and leg will extend on the side to which the head is turned, while the arm and leg on the opposite side flex. This is the ATNR and it should be activated when a baby is placed on his or her tummy and the face turns automatically to one side to enable breathing to take place. As the head moves to one side, so the baby's eyes follow the hand in the same direction, with the head, eyes, and hand moving in unison. Eventually, the baby's eye and hand movements begin to happen independent of the head movement, which is an early sign of hand–eye coordination (Goddard Blythe, 2005a; McPhillips et al., 2000) and this is very important for later literacy development and other aspects of coordination.

Constant rehearsal and repetition of reflex movements is vital for their integration and the infant's development (McPhillips et al., 2000). However McPhillips et al. (2000) and Goddard Blythe (2005a) have also found that when the ATNR persists in primary age children, then it not only hinders the development of balance and coordination but can also affect later reading and writing skills.

The Palmar reflex is particularly noticeable when a baby's grasp on an adult's finger is strong enough to enable the baby to be pulled into an upright position. This reflex is connected to feeding, as the infant might grasp the finger of an adult when sucking milk or else an adult can stroke a newborn baby's palm to encourage it to suck when it is reluctant to. The fingers and thumb work together until this reflex becomes more refined so the infant can move each finger independently and is eventually able to manipulate objects. Interestingly the fingers, though smaller in size than other body parts, take up a large number of the neurons in the motor cortex because of the precision of the movement that the fingers need to make (Greenfield, 2001: 132). The mouth too takes up a considerable share of this part of the brain in order to undertake the complex task of speech development. Goddard Blythe (2005a: 59) has assessed children with speech difficulties who also have 'difficulty with thumb and finger opposition as well as with hypersensitivity to gentle stimulation to the palm of the hand'.

The numerous early primary reflexes drive the baby to move, stimulating lower functions of the brain so that, after much practice, the infant is able to 'sit, roll over, tummy crawl, crawl on all fours, develop a pincer grip and eventually stand and walk' (Goddard Blythe, 2005a: 63-64). As the infant grows and matures, early reflexes are gradually controlled to allow more mature postural reflexes to develop. During the first three-and-a-half years, postural reflexes enable the child to move more fluidly by gaining control of the body, posture and body movements. This is an important stage of development for a child whose brain is functioning efficiently.

The positive interplay of genes, the environment, and interactions can enable children to reach significant movement milestones in their development. If, however, a child encounters interruptions in development for whatever reason, then it is likely to indicate that learning difficulties will appear later.

The seven senses

The senses in the body drive young infants to explore the world around them. Newborn babies immediately respond to their new environment through their senses. So, for instance, they will sense leaving the warmth of the womb and feel the air on their skin, then the water when being washed and the loving arms of their parents when held, and attempt to gain eye contact with their mothers while breastfeeding and hear soothing noises being made by their parents.

The five senses of taste, smell, touch, vision and hearing are generally well known and acknowledged to be important aspects of young children's development. The vestibular and proprioception are two less well-known senses, though they are connected to the five senses.

The vestibular system is primarily responsible for balance, while proprioception tells us where our bodies are in space and helps us to know where parts of our body are in relation to each other.

The vestibular system

It is constant motion that activates the vestibular system. This sense is stimulated in the womb, as the mother moves around, and later, after birth, as the infant is gently rocked to and fro. This type of motion provides input for the vestibular system, which, eventually, enables the body to learn how to control movement and balance. This system enables young children to maintain body postures, which is vital for everything they will do in their daily lives (Hannaford, 1995).

As the balance system develops it supports infants in maintaining stable postures. Infants learn to sit up when their back muscles are strong enough and when the balance function of the inner ear is more fully developed. This is important as, when children are older, they need to have a stable posture in order to sit upright to write, copy from the board, type or listen to the teacher.

Children whose vestibular sense is functioning well will feel confident with their internal balance system and respond to vigorous vestibular activity with enjoyment. They will want to be up and active throughout the day, looking to take part in spinning, swinging, rocking, falling and tumbling activities, and will be able to perform 'remarkable feats of balance' (Hannaford, 1995: 36).

Coordination, balance and movement rely on a vestibular system that is functioning well. Indications that children are experiencing problems with balance may be seen if they have difficulty standing, walking, running, or climbing the stairs without falling or bumping into things, stumbling or tripping. A child may find walking on uneven surfaces awkward, appearing to be uncoordinated and clumsy, but may be experiencing difficulties with balance. Resolving balance problems can bring about a significant improvement to the overall quality of a child's life and his or her ability to play and learn (Macintyre and McVitty, 2004).

There is a strong link between the vestibular system and vision, which controls eye movements so that objects are in focus as the body moves. Any problems with this may affect a child's ability to follow an object with the eyes when the body is moving (Hannaford, 1995).

By activating the vestibular system, children will stimulate their brains so that they are open to learning. The brain and body are connected and cannot be regarded separately. The vestibular system is also closely associated with touch and proprioception.

Proprioception – the sixth sense

Proprioceptors can be found in the muscles and joints and are activated by bodily movement, letting us know where each part of our body is in relation to the rest, how it is moving, and where our bodies are in space (Hannaford, 1995). If the proprioceptive system is in good working order, then children will thrive when engaged in physical activity and be willing participants in movement-play. In infants, proprioception works together with vision, touch and the vestibular system to support them in their drive to reach developmental milestones, such as rolling over, crawling and walking.

If this system is not working well, then the body can be floppy or children may have difficulties sensing the position of their own limbs. They may seek out active movements, such as pushing, pulling, rough and tumble, strong bear hugs or being sandwiched between two cushions, anything that gives them the vigorous proprioceptive input they need (Kranowitz, 2005: 142).

Sacks (2007: 58), a neurologist and psychiatrist, writes about his patients' neurological disorders, referring to the proprioceptive system as the 'vital sixth sense', without which a human being is 'disembodied'. He refers to his patient Christina, who is unable to 'feel' her body parts or that her body belongs to her. She lost her sense of proprioception and became like a floppy doll. Christina's condition is very rare, however – the more commonly seen indications of an under-responsive system include having a fairly floppy or weak posture or not being aware of where different body parts are.

A child whose posture may be described as floppy, whose legs are not strong enough to stand and whose spine is not able to hold the upper body up for sitting independently must be encouraged to continue tummy time and crawling until the body is aligned and the muscles have strengthened sufficiently that they are ready to hold the body in an upright posture (Lamont, 2014). Difficulties related to this system are some of the hardest and most frustrating for a child to live with, and further help from medical professionals may be needed.

A vast amount of sensory input is received by each young child, which the brain then processes and coordinates and, ultimately, the body expresses as movement (Greenfield, 2001). All sensory systems, in order to be able to function well, work in collaboration with each other, which means that if a problem occurs in one system, a multitude of difficulties can arise (Macintyre and McVitty, 2004).

Movement patterns

Those living or working with young children will have noticed that they love to move and they move instinctively, as their bodies just tell them to. As we have seen so far, infants' early reflex movements and senses are driving forth the growth of their brains to their full potential; later, children will seek out specific developmental movement activities. Yet, the natural tendency for young children to move tends to be taken for granted rather than fully appreciated for the impact it has on their development.

Tummy time

As babies move on their tummies, with their arms and legs working together to propel them forwards, this movement pattern helps to develop their stability and mobility (Lamont, 2007b). Many other skills are emerging as babies push up the upper body, showing incredible strength as their arms hold them away from the floor. This is the groundwork for developing the upright posture as this movement aligns the cervical and lumbar spine. At the same time, as infants move their heads from left to right and right to left, the eyes track horizontally – a skill needed in later years to read (Lamont, 2007b). Tummy crawling 'creates a range of motions in the hip sockets and shoulders' that eventually improve the organisation of these joints (Lamont, 2007b: 2). Lamont found that children who had lots of tummy time, which stimulates the pelvic area, were more likely to be ready for toilet training 'on time', whereas many of those preschool and older children who missed out on tummy time experienced difficulty with toilet training still at those later ages. Also, as infants hold themselves up, their hands and arms rotate in this position, enabling fine motor skills to begin to emerge. This stage of development gives infants time to develop an awareness and organisation of their lower body through much practice and hard work (Lamont, 2007b).

This is a vital developmental stage for young infants, yet many have had little or no time on their tummies (Lamont, 2007b; Mcintyre and McVitty, 2004). This is the position all infants between ten weeks and seven months should be in unless they are sleeping or being held by an adult (Lamont, 2007b). Given the space, time and opportunities to repeat and practise a number of intricate movements at this stage, infants will eventually reach the stage of the crawling pattern.

Crawling

Crawling is a milestone in infants' development; it is the first time they are up off the floor, conquering gravity and laying the foundations for balance that will be with them for the rest of their lives (Lamont, 2007b: 2).

When crawling on hands and knees, both hemispheres of the brain communicate and interchange information with each other through the corpus collosum (Lamont, 2007b). Thus, crawling creates neurological connections between the two hemispheres, so the more a baby crawls, the faster these connections will transmit information. This movement also helps the spine to align and the shoulders and hips further rotate in preparation for walking (Lamont, 2007b).

Crawling on hands and knees combines balance, vision, touch and proprioception. Visual convergence is stimulated as infants look up and down, focusing on things at varying distances while crawling. As they crawl, their hands open out on the floor, strengthening fine motor movements that eventually can become, in time and with practice, 'the skilled and dexterous movements of a pianist' (Greenfield, 2001: 44). 'Fine motor movements are controlled by the motor cortex which communicates with other parts of the brain in order to activate the finger muscles' (Greenfield, 2001: 44). Indeed, the neurological development that is taking place here is laying the foundations for later tasks, such as passing an object from one hand to another, and, later still in their development, taking notes in class.

The first year of an infant's life is truly very busy indeed! Each movement pattern provides the foundations for the next phase, stimulating innumerable functions. Without the experience of early movement patterns, it is likely that there will be some degree of developmental delay. Interestingly, Lamont (2007b: 3) found that when these early movement patterns were undertaken by older children in a therapy programme, they led to 'improvements in visual motor skills, tracking, balance, impulse control, anger management, reading and attention'.

Further movement activities

During children's first six to eight years, the growth of their brains and neurological system is dependent on them working hard at stimulating the nervous system through movement activities, such as tummy crawling, crawling on all fours, running, tumbling, spinning, swinging, pushing, pulling and hanging upside down (Lamont, 2007d).

These movements involve the complex coordination of muscle groups linked to the brain stem (Greenfield, 2001). Young children's future achievements are dependent on their movement experiences from the time they are born as these cause the brain to 'constantly transform itself in unimaginably plastic ways' (Hannaford, 1995: 14). The brain's structure is connected to young children's inner body mechanisms, driving movements that ultimately restructure the architecture of the brain. Throughout children's early years, their engagement in specific movement patterns stimulates the neurological system so that 'the body becomes the instrument of learning' (Hannaford, 1995: 18).

Examples of children engaged in significant movement patterns can be seen in Chapter 3.

CASE STUDY

Amir was three years and six months old and had attended 1a Children's Centre full-time since he was three years old. His parents and staff were becoming increasingly concerned about his habit of biting children, which was happening more and more. This increase in biting was of such concern to his parents, especially his father who travelled a lot on business and was often away from home for long periods of time, that they began to hint they might withdraw Amir from the Centre. The Centre's Head, Marilyn Sherwood-Chilton, met with Amir's parents and, with their permission, discussed their concerns with Bette Lamont, a developmental movement consultant from Seattle, who was working with the local authority at that time.

Amir was a delightful boy who eagerly joined in with activities presented in the nursery for all the children. As time progressed, however, what became his habitual biting of other children prevented them from playing with him. His lower face was limp and his tongue tended to hang out of his mouth and he often dribbled. Concern was also rising about his language development as communication was extremely limited with both peers and staff.

Assessment

An informal assessment from a neurological perspective by Bette Lamont revealed that Amir was in a state of under-responsiveness, with low muscle tone and poor sensation in his face. Bette also observed that he had an 'overall awkwardness, poor body awareness and lowered sensations generally, which were leading him to some of his unsociable behaviours'.

From a neurological viewpoint, Bette Lamont's analysis revealed that nerves in Amir's face were under-responsive through a lack of stimulation and his awkward, uncoordinated gait indicated he had missed out on the usual crawling pattern, which was later confirmed by his parents.

As Amir held on to the scooter during his assessment, his hands were shaped in a 'grasp' that looked like the Palmar reflex. This reflex is normally inhibited gradually in the first six to seven months of life, beginning with the ability to let go of an object, such as a favourite toy. Interestingly, the Palmar reflex has a connection to the mouth and feeding – as gentle pressure is applied to the palm of the hands, an infant can be encouraged to start sucking (Goddard Blythe, 2005).

Lack of control of his mouth and saliva escaping, together with using his hands in a fist, indicated that the Palmar reflex was possibly still present for Amir. While the Palmar reflex remains, with the thumb and four fingers continuing to operate together, a child is unable to acquire good fine motor skills, which will enable him or her to develop a pincer grip and manipulate objects, for instance. Lack of articulation of the hands and mouth was of particular interest in Amir's case as this is crucial for speech development.

Intervention

Interventions for Amir included massaging his face with different textures. His Key Person at the Children's Centre, Sharon Sparkes, set up a box together with Amir, who chose a variety of scratchy, soft, cool and smooth implements with which to massage his face, such as a sponge, an emery board, a smooth pebble, a feather and Velcro, which he kept inside this box. He would willingly undertake this task himself or invite an adult to choose an item to use on his face while he continued to play with the sand, for example.

The nervous system can be stimulated by activities related to the proprioception system, such as pressing firmly on to the body with cushions below and on top of the child's body. The Centre Head introduced this activity to the children, which resulted in a queue of children waiting for their turn as it seemed such fun. It was called the 'sandwich'!

Crawling activities were also introduced, among other things, to align Amir's gait, as well as encourage the opening of his hands and fingers, which assists with the inhibition of this reflex so that he would be able to develop good manual dexterity before he transitioned from nursery to school.

Outcome

The number of times a day Amir was biting dramatically decreased and he stopped biting altogether within the first two weeks of the

(Continued)

(Continued)

start of the intervention. As mentioned previously, Amir's parents had thought about withdrawing him from the Centre, but they changed their minds when they saw how much happier he was and how much his social interactions with peers had improved.

Amir also stopped dribbling and his language improved, as did his communication with others and his behaviour. Consequently, he was able to make friends as his behaviour matured through the work carried out on his sensory system.

When Bette was given this feedback about Amir's progress since her intervention, she said, 'It is amazing to hear about Amir's success, and with such a short intervention on my part and such a simple intervention on the part of the nursery. I bet his parents are very proud of him and grateful to the nursery. I guess it was just all in him and we just had to do a few things to unlock it.'

Conclusion

Goddard Blythe (2005b) questions whether or not every child is ready for school in terms of their neuro-motor development, which describes a range of physical skills, including balance, posture and coordination. If these physical foundations for learning are secured in the preschool years, then children enter the school system better equipped to cope with the demands of the classroom, such as the ability to sit and concentrate, coordinate their hand and eyes when writing and control the eye movements needed for reading. Goddard Blythe has found that some children appear to be readier than others when they start school.

One way to address this situation would be to ensure that all infants and young children are provided with opportunities for movement-play activities. Early education settings need to 'create the best possible environment to support the child's unfolding mind and complex brain' for all children in preschools and in early primary school from birth to six or seven years of age (Lamont, 2007b).

Further reading

Bette Lamont's website, for various resources, at: http://neurologicalreorganization. org/resources/

Goddard Blythe, S. (2005a) *The Well Balanced Child: Movement and early learning* (Second Edition). Stroud: Hawthorne Press.

Goddard Blythe, S. (2005b) *Reflexes, Learning and Behaviour: A window into the child's mind: A non-invasive approach to solving learning & behavior problems.* Eugene, OR: Fern Ridge Press.

Greenfield, S. (2001) *The Human Brain: A guided tour* (Reissue). London: Phoenix.

Hannaford, C. (1995) *Smart Moves: Why learning is not all in your head.* Weaverville: Great Ocean Publishers.

Kranowitz, C. (2005) *The Out-of-Sync Child: Recognizing and coping with sensory processing disorder* (Revised). New York: Skylight Press, Perigee Books.

Maude, P. (2010) 'Physical literacy and the young child'. AIESEP Conference Paper.

McPhillips, M., Hepper, P.G. and Mulhern, G. (2000) 'Effects of replicating primary-reflex movements on specific reading difficulties in children: A randomised, double-blind, controlled trial'. *The Lancet*, 355: 537–41.

Rutter, M. (2006a) *Genes and Behavior: Nature–nurture interplay explained.* Malden, MA: Blackwell.

Sacks, O. (2007) *The Man Who Mistook His Wife for a Hat.* London: Picador.

The Royal Society (TRS) (2011) 'Brain Waves Module 2: Neuroscience: implications for education and lifelong learning'. RS Policy document 02/11, DES2105. London: The Royal Society.

2
Making the case for physical activity

Introduction

This chapter's focus is on the health benefits of physical activity for young children. Good health is considered to be one of the most important determinants of a child's life chances, yet the combination of changes in dietary patterns and lower physical activity has resulted in critical and worrying increases in childhood obesity. For the first time, therefore, physical activity for young children from birth has been considered by the chief medical officers (CMOs) in the UK (DH, 2011). The amount of time infants, children and adults should be physically active has been stipulated, with evidence given for its overall health benefits. At the same time, an investigation into actual levels of children's physical activity found that, in preschool and the first year of school, young children are too sedentary (Evangelou et al., 2009). With increasing numbers of infants and young children spending time in early childhood provision, these settings could provide a suitable point of intervention to increase physical activity levels.

Physical development is one of the key domains of child development and learning for young children, as seen in the early years curriculum in England (DfE, 2014). The Department for Education (DfE, 2014: 8) recognises the importance of physical development in a child's early years, emphasising that, 'Children must be helped to understand the importance of physical activity and to make healthy choices in relation to food'.

Physical development involves opportunities for young children to be active and interactive; to develop their coordination, control and movement. Movement-play is at the heart of physical development for infants and young children and this is inextricably linked to other domains of a child's development, including physical, cognitive, social and emotional development, communication and self-regulation, as outlined in Chapter 1.

Physical development is a key component of the curriculum for all four countries in the UK and part of the curriculum in most international curricula guidance documents.

The acknowledgement of physical development as a vital component of children's development requires theory and research to be brought together to inform better teaching and learning practices. Despite these endeavours by policymakers, Evangelou et al. (2009) and Archer and Siraj (2015) reveal that physical activity is not equally applied to all young children in all EYFS provision. This leads to the crucial role that adults play in providing an enabling environment and ensuring each child has equal and good access to opportunities to become a physically confident, competent and capable mover.

Obesity *is* preventable!

Increasing numbers of young children are reported to be obese. This phenomenon is not unique to the UK; it is also reported worldwide. The World Health Organization (WHO) (2013) reports that obesity has doubled worldwide since 1980.

The WHO (2013) highlights that '65% of the world's population live in countries where overweight or obesity kills more people than underweight'. In 2011, over 40 million children under the age of five were overweight (WHO, 2013). A study (Canning et al., 2004) conducted in Newfoundland and Labrador, Canada, found that 25.6 per cent, which is 1 in 4, preschool-aged children were overweight or obese. Nationwide data in the USA show that the percentage of obese children aged 2 to 5 years increased more than 30 per cent between 2001 and 2004 (McWilliams et al., 2009). Figures from the Department of Health (2011) in the UK show that over a fifth of children are either overweight or obese by the time they join reception class aged between four and five years in primary schools in England.

This dramatic increase in the number of people who are overweight or obese in the world makes it the fifth leading risk for global deaths (WHO, 2013). The WHO (2013) reports that chronic diseases such as diabetes, heart disease and stroke, musculoskeletal disorders and certain cancers are attributable to being overweight. The Department of Health (2013) estimates that the costs to health services in the UK of treating patients who present with illnesses related to obesity total more than £5 billion every year, though the economic costs worldwide are considered to be vast (Hillman et al., 2008).

Fundamentally, the usual cause of being overweight is an imbalance in energy, between calories consumed and calories expended (WHO, 2013). Being overweight or obese with the related diseases is largely preventable (WHO, 2013: 4) by limiting the intake of some fats, sugar and salt. It is the combination of dietary patterns *and* lower physical activity levels, however, that has led to this critical increase in childhood obesity. Physical inactivity and sedentary behaviours will be discussed in more depth later.

It is important to also remember that some children are undernourished in the world, including in the UK. It is therefore also important to achieve a balance between healthy nutrition and activity. Luckily, very young children are naturally active and physical, so we are pushing at an open door. The adults who work with young children need to model these behaviours of healthy living and movement.

It is through action at national, regional and local levels that problems of inequality should be addressed, in order to improve diets generally and increase physical activity patterns in the population as a whole (WHO, 2013). At a national level, this is being done by the Children's Food Trust (formerly the School Food Trust), endorsed by the government and the early years sector. The Trust has produced the 'Eat Better, Start Better' training programme (Children's Food Trust, 2012), at the heart of which is its 'Voluntary food and drink guidelines for early years settings in England'. Also, the Caroline Walker Trust has produced comprehensive guides on food and nutrition for children under five years of age, which are available at: www.cwt.org.uk.

The four chief medical officers (DH, 2011), from the four home countries in the UK, have provided new and revised recommendations for physical activity at a national level. These are outlined later in this chapter.

Changes in dietary patterns leading to obesity accompanied by physical inactivity and increasing sedentary behaviours are seriously affecting young children's health. Worryingly, obese children have a higher chance of being obese in adulthood, which can lead to premature death and disability in adulthood (WHO, 2013). Concern is rising about childhood obesity because of health issues such as breathing difficulties, an increased risk of fractures, hypertension, early markers of cardiovascular disease, insulin resistance and psychological effects that do not usually emerge before adulthood (WHO, 2013).

Alongside dietary changes, an increase in regular physical exercise is needed to improve children's health and well-being. A general consensus among health officials in the USA, Canada, Australia and the UK is that the early years are 'one of the critical periods in the establishment of sedentary and physical activity behaviours' (Reilly et al., 2006: 5).

Early childhood settings therefore have a vital role to play in young children's future life chances.

Children attending early education settings

Many young children across the world attend a range of early childhood settings, including compulsory schooling, children's centres, preschools, playgroups, kindergartens, day nurseries and childcare provision, as well as childminders or family daycare or are perhaps looked after by relatives. No country has one universal type of early childhood setting catering for the needs of all infants and young children from birth to six years of age, but significant numbers of them are attending childhood provision of some kind. For instance, Tucker et al. (2011), looking at physical activity in such settings, found that 54 per cent of preschool children in Canada attend childcare.

The numbers of children attending early childhood provision have increased significantly in the UK, too, over the last few years. For example, the Department for Education (2012) reported that full-time day-care places increased by 33 per cent between 2007 and 2011. In January 2012, 96 per cent of the population of three- and four-year-olds accessed their free entitlement to early education (DfE, 2012). Increasing provision is currently sought for two-year-olds as part of the government's drive to offer free places to the least advantaged. Since September 2014, 40 per cent of two-year-olds from disadvantaged families are entitled to government funding to secure a place at a nursery or school for 15 hours each week (DfE, 2012). In response, primary schools in the UK are increasingly opening new classes for two-year-olds as well as nursery classes, with reception classes continuing the foundation stage curriculum.

With such increasing numbers of young children attending early childhood education and schools at a critical time in their development, these settings could provide a suitable intervention in terms of levels of physical activity. All such settings have a responsibility to ensure that all the children are provided with a varied and healthy diet while in their care and make a commitment to follow recommendations made by the chief medical officers on physical activity levels and reductions in sedentary behaviours. Heads and managers need to communicate this information to staff, parents and children. Communication can then be followed up with 'concerted action' at all levels to 'create environments and conditions that make it easier for children to be active'

(DH, 2011: 10). This chapter will help those interested in reflecting on their current provision and policy. Developing a physical development policy will be further explored in Chapter 6.

Enabling environments and the role of the adult

It is incumbent on us all to ensure children are provided with the conditions required for them to be physically active and we need to seek out spaces indoors, outdoors, green and urban in which this can happen. An environment in which children learn and develop is one that offers stimulating resources and rich learning opportunities through play that encourages them to take risks and explore. In this environment, adults play a central role in providing a mix of adult-led and child-initiated activities, ensuring a balance between activities led by children and those led or guided by staff (DfE, 2014: 9). This balance is vital when children are physically active if they are to 'play constructively and generate their own games and physical play', as adults extend the children's interests through interactions and create 'some structure or facilitate play by providing enabling environments' (DH, 2011: 22).

Indeed, studies (Archer and Siraj, 2015; Evangelou et al., 2009) have shown that adult intervention is vital if infants and young children are to increase their levels of physical activity. Clearly there is a consensus between health officials, policymakers and researchers that adults have an important role to fulfil, providing an enriched environment and engaging with children in their physical activity.

Nonetheless, researchers (Archer and Siraj, 2015; Brown et al., 2009; Evangelou et al., 2009; Sigmund et al., 2009) have found that practitioners rarely prompt children to increase or decrease their level of physical activity and this is clearly a huge drawback, working counter to the recommendations of the chief medical officers and good early years pedagogy. Indeed, the Statutory Guidance for the EYFS in England, setting the standards for education and care, is quite clear that practitioners are expected to focus strongly on physical development alongside other prime areas. Young children's physical activity is, however, rarely found to be vigorous or even moderate (Brown et al., 2009) and this, disturbingly, indicates that there is a gap between policy and practice.

Furthermore, the chief medical officers' report (DH, 2011) highlights the importance of physical stimulation for children's health, which is being seriously compromised by inactivity and sedentary behaviours. Research mentioned previously reminds us that adult intervention and the adult role are important in children's experiences in early childhood settings. Staff in early years provision clearly must take action!

The importance of sustained interactions

Vygotsky's socio-constructivist theory has influenced thinking about how children learn and, consequently, what pedagogies it is appropriate to apply. The adult, in Vygotsky's (1978) theory, plays a significant role in the child's zone of proximal development (ZPD). Vygotsky defined ZPD as, 'The distance between the actual developmental level as determined by independent problem solving and the level of potential development as determined through problem solving under adult guidance, or in collaboration with more capable peers' (A 1978: 86). This means that the adult's role, according to Vygotsky, is to assist the child in their playful exploration in order to extend and enhance their learning (Siraj-Blatchford, 2009). This can also be achieved between peers.

A current and significant contribution to understanding pedagogical practice and its influence on the 'emergent development' of the child comes from analysis of the Effective Provision of Pre-school Education (EPPE) Project (Sylva et al., 2004). A general pattern of improved cognitive outcomes was found to be associated with sustained adult–child verbal interactions. Coining the phrase 'sustained shared thinking' (SST), Siraj-Blatchford (2009: 1) defines such interactions as 'an effective pedagogic interaction, where two or more individuals "work together" in an intellectual way to solve a problem, clarify a concept, evaluate activities, or extend a narrative'. Thus, children who have plenty of sustained shared interactions with adults or peers were found to benefit intellectually and socially from this. Siraj-Blatchford (2009: 1) further notes the 'educational potential of shared playful activities' as they provide children with opportunities to sustain such interactions.

Sustained movement conversations

Playful interactions between adults and children and a child and another child were observed in a study carried out by ourselves (Archer and Siraj, 2015) during movement-play activities in which we witnessed periods of sustained movement conversations. Such interactions were identified, for example, when peers moved together, exploring their own body potential, concentrating and persisting as they encountered new movements, extending their ideas and enjoying their achievements together.

CASE STUDY

A number of boys in a nursery class on a very wet day showed high energy levels while confined indoors. After discussions with the class teacher, appropriate resources, such as mats and cushions, were provided in order to encourage free movement in a safe environment. These resources were set out in an inviting way for the children.

One child chose to fall on to the cushions, tumble over and roll. Another child, observing her peer, copied these movements and then they both tumbled and rolled independent of each other. After a short while, they were interacting, rolling and tumbling with each other and over each other. More children quickly joined them in their movement-play, adding to the repertoire of movement experiences, such as forward rolls and somersaults. The teacher joined the children in this activity.

As the children all rough and tumbled together, they sustained movement conversations, extending their range of movements. The children became deeply involved in this activity, while showing enjoyment through smiles and laughter.

Panksepp (1998: 287) claims that it is easy to recognise when children are enjoying this activity by their smiles and laughter, which express their 'mood' and 'sense of camaraderie'. Such play and laughter, Panksepp suggests, serve the function of social bonding and the sensory system of touch also has a role to play in instigating and sustaining such social play.

Prior to the situation described above, rough and tumble play was neither available nor acceptable at this early childhood setting. The teacher had not heard of it and the setting had not considered it appropriate. Once resources were available, however, the three- and four-year-olds involved in this activity practised their skills in tumbling alone and with each other, acquiring knowledge of their body potential and developing new attitudes towards what became acceptable, physically active play in their classroom. In this way, the adult considered the provision of resources in relation to the emerging development of the children and joined them in this activity, too.

The children learned how to move in relation to each other in collaborative physical play, scaffolding for each other within their 'zones of capability' (Siraj-Blatchford, 2009: 8). Less confident children, when working with a competent peer, extended their capabilities to include activities they could successfully accomplish with peer support. In this way, children were provided with opportunities to sustain and share interactions through this movement activity that was spontaneous, but could also be more structured. Essentially, the children move forward in their development through these types of play activities (Vygotsky, 1978).

Rough and tumble play helps children to develop their physical fitness, their strength and self-control. As children rough and tumble together, they learn what is right or wrong, what is acceptable behaviour and about resolving conflicts (Goddard Blythe, 2005a). We know through anecdotal evidence that many fathers enjoy rough and tumbling with their children. This playful activity provides opportunities to strengthen the bonds between adult and child or child and child.

The vital role of the adult can be undertaken to take the children's development forward: 'Left to their own devices we know that the play of children often becomes repetitive, and effective educators therefore need to encourage children to take on new challenges and introduce new and extended experiences' (Siraj-Blatchford, 2009: 10). Indeed, we found in our study (Archer and Siraj, 2015) that adults played a crucial role in developing the children's movement experiences. After movement-play training, adults more willingly took part in movement activities with children, which led to them expanding their movement repertoire and this sometimes resulted in children engaging in more challenging physical activity. This study is discussed more fully in Chapter 4.

The Early Years Foundation Stage (EYFS)

The Statutory Framework for the Early Years Foundation Stage (EYFS) sets the standards that all early childhood providers in England must meet to ensure that children learn and develop well and are kept healthy and safe (DfE, 2014). The Framework includes a requirement for the provision of healthy, balanced and nutritious food and drink (DfE, 2014: 26).

The Framework also places a stronger emphasis, than did previous Frameworks, on communication and language, personal, social and emotional development and physical development, now considered to be prime curriculum areas crucial to 'igniting children's curiosity and enthusiasm for learning, and for building their capacity to learn, form relationships and thrive' (DfE, 2014: 7). These prime areas are undoubtedly interconnected with each other.

Practitioners are 'expected to focus strongly on these three prime areas', which are considered to be 'the basis of successful learning' (DfE, 2014: 8). With regard to physical development, this curriculum area is seen as a route through which young children develop and learn and become 'ready for school' (DfE, 2014: 9). In this way, policy and research are providing the same message, but there appears to be a gap between policy and practice, as research shows that young children are not as active as they should be. This gap needs to close and it is adults who could make a difference in making this happen.

The Framework places emphasis on the practitioner's role, with the practitioner being expected to 'plan purposeful play through a mix of adult-led and child-initiated activity' (DfE, 2014: 9). Yet, research has revealed that adults rarely intervened in children's physical activity, resulting in low levels of physically active play. Practitioners can, however, make a real difference to children's engagement in physical activity and support them to increase their levels through encouragement, by following their lead and responding to their innovative ways of moving.

Guidelines for physical activity

As stated earlier, the chief medical officers have noted that physical inactivity and sedentary behaviours are being established during the critical period of early childhood. Regular physical activity is the key to reducing many chronic health conditions and improving mental health and musculosketel conditions (DH, 2011). It is crucial, therefore, that, from birth, children develop behaviours that lead to greater physical activity and less sedentary behaviour. To this end, the chief medical officers have produced new guidelines for physical activity. This is the first time that collaboration has taken place on a national scale and consistency has been established across the four home countries on the amount and type of physical activity we should all aim to do at each stage of our lives.

The report (DH, 2011) reflects the latest scientific global evidence from the UK, Australia, USA and Canada, with a view to informing changes in behaviour. These changes, the report claims, must be led by a nationwide policy of dissemination and implementation. It is not clear how this is to be achieved, however. This book therefore aims to contribute towards these two aims by making this knowledge available and detailing the practical implementation of physical movement activities in Chapters 3 and 4.

New guidelines on physical activity for young children can be found in 'Start Active, Stay Active: A report on physical activity from the four home countries' Chief Medical Officers' (DH, 2011). The details of this report are discussed further in Chapter 6.

Guidelines for early years settings

Under fives

1. Physical activity should be encouraged from birth, particularly through floor based-play and water-based activities in safe environments.
2. Children of preschool age who are capable of walking unaided should be physically active daily for at least 180 minutes (3 hours), spread throughout the day.
3. All under fives should minimise the amount of time spent being sedentary (being restrained or sitting) for extended periods (except time spent sleeping).

(DH, 2011: 20)

The chief medical officers (CMOs) in the UK state there is good scientific evidence that being physically active can help us lead healthier and happier lives. Guidelines written by the CMOs (DH, 2011: 10) 'apply across the population, irrespective of gender, race or socio-economic status'. The information below is taken from this report and set out in boxes and charts that early childhood settings may wish to use in displays or policies.

From birth, not yet walking unaided

The consensus of the CMOs and movement specialists is that physical activity is central to a baby's normal growth and development. For those infants who are not yet walking, it is essential to provide space for them to crawl, play and roll around on the floor in the months immediately following birth until they are walking confidently. Water-based activities for parents and babies are also recommended.

Infants not yet walking need space to play, wearing unrestrictive clothing to enable them to move their legs and arms, reach for and grasp objects, turn their heads towards stimuli, pull and push and play with other people. Space needs to be uncluttered for infants to move with objects that are just out of reach to encourage them to move and roll over towards them.

Infants need as much time as necessary to learn new movements, such as using large muscles for kicking, rolling, pushing up to crawling, pulling to a standing position and, eventually, walking. Infants who are reluctant movers need to feel the rhythm of movement in their bodies as adults hold them in their arms while they spin and dance or safely toss them in the air.

All this development takes time and infants need to rehearse these movements repeatedly until they are capable and competent movers.

Infants' physical activity

Reaching for objects	Kicking legs
Grasping objects	Crawling on tummy
Turning head towards stimuli	Crawling on all fours
Pulling	Pulling up to standing
Pushing	Walking
Playing with other people	Swimming

Sedentary behaviours

Sedentary behaviours must be limited to aid infants' health and development. These include being seated or lying down, watching TV, travelling by car, bus or train, being strapped in a buggy, carry seat, baby bouncer and so on. In fact, any such container that restricts babies' movements so that they spend a large proportion of time being sedentary will act as a barrier to their physical activity. Establishing healthy patterns of behaviour is important at this time to ensure a healthy life for the present and in their future. Minimising the amount of time all children under five years of age spend being sedentary is recommended by the CMOs – we should encourage movement.

CASE STUDY

An infant started at our early childhood centre aged 13 months. He was quiet and passive, able to sit up independently, though not yet freely moving from one spot in the room to another.

We have met many infants of various ages who are able to sit upright yet not move around by themselves. Often infants at this stage of development are used to being carried from one place to another. It is crucial, however, that infants who tend to be fairly passive and immobile feel a sense of movement within themselves. Adults will need to find ingenious ways to help young children experience this feeling of movement by rocking them gently or dancing with them in their arms or pulling them gently along the floor on a piece of material. The floor is the first playground for infants, whether they are on their tummies or backs; it is where crucial development takes place as they roll from their backs to their tummies and vice versa.

We put this infant on his tummy, a few minutes at a time at first, increasing the time each day and trying different ways to achieve this – on a body ball or rolling cushion and, of course, being down on our tummies on the floor with him. After much practice, being on his tummy and learning to move on his tummy, this infant then pushed himself up using his arms and hands, raising himself off the floor, and eventually crawled on all fours.

These early movement patterns are vital to all infants' growth and development, supporting motor skills, balance and posture for when they are ready to stand upright.

Preschool children, walking unaided

The CMOs recommend that children who are capable of walking unaided at preschool should be physically active daily for a minimum of 180 minutes (3 hours). This should not be taken all at the same time, but spread throughout the day. This is a minimum – young children need to be physically active on a regular basis for even more time than this to benefit from additional health gains. A gradual increase in physical activity is recommended for children under five years who have been very inactive.

The young child emerging from floor-based play to walking unaided requires unstructured, active and energetic play. These children will need to be active several hours a day to develop their fundamental movement skills and master their physical environment. New physical activity guidelines recommend that children have the 'freedom to create their own opportunities for active play, direct their own play and engage in imaginative play' (DH, 2011: 22). Similarly, optimal early years practice is based on sound principles of play and active learning, putting the child at the heart of practice.

Outdoor play

The outdoor environment provides a non-threatening context for infants and young children to learn about their world. Young children need daily access to the outdoors, with appropriate footwear and clothing for all weathers. Children need an environment that inspires them to learn, where they can take risks, explore, experiment, build dens, play with natural materials, move and be physically active. Being outdoors, in touch with the natural world, where children can, for example, dig, plant and learn about daisies, buttercups, tadpoles and frogs, ensures that they develop a love for the natural world. A small pile of logs or a fallen tree can support a multitude of different insects – woodlice, beetles; fungi and plant life. Logs provide these creatures with a home and food that will attract prey, such as spiders, frogs, toads and birds. A flourishing wildlife community that can exist on logs and fallen trees encourages curious children to explore, learn from and be delighted by what they discover.

Logs can also be a means for children to travel, jumping from one to another, judging distances and testing balancing skills as they go. Fallen trees provide young children with climbing opportunities, from where they can jump to ground level from various points. Children enjoy physical challenges as they create dens from ropes, branches and materials, using their creativity and imagination with open-ended resources. 'Outdoors' includes gardens, playgrounds, parks, adventure playgrounds and fields, for example. Adventurous and vigorous physical activity stimulates the neurological system, develops the young child's ability to problem solve and take risks, and improves their confidence and health.

The consequences of reduced physical activity are low skill levels and low movement competence, which are a major barrier to participation in sport (Hands and Martin, 2003). Furthermore, children with low motor competence tend to be active less often, spend less time playing and interacting with their peers, and play less on playground equipment (Bouffard et al., 1996). This is further evidence that movement skills are vital for children's learning and development. Moreover, Evangelou et al. (2009: 72) found in their review that a 'lack of confidence and competence in performing these skills can have detrimental effects on children's social and emotional wellbeing'.

Levels of physical activity

Despite the young child's innate urge to move and be active, Evangelou et al. (2009) in their review of studies investigating physical activity levels at nursery and the first year of school revealed alarming levels of inactivity for young children. One such piece of research by Sigmund et al. (2009: 77) investigated children and their physical activity levels in preschool and the first year of school in the Czech Republic, where the age of children at preschool is five, and in the first year at school, six. The researchers made use of a pedometer to measure daily the number of steps taken and an accelerometer to calculate energy expenditure. Children in their first year at school were found to be significantly less active than preschool children on weekdays, during time spent at school, and at weekends.

More disturbing are the findings Brown et al. (2009) disclosed about young children's physical activity levels. It is important to remember that infants and young children today are spending a large proportion of their time in early education and daycare settings where active play should be routine. One US study, however, set in a childcare centre, showed that 89 per cent of children's time was spent being sedentary (Brown et al., 2009). Levels of physical activity for preschool children in this study reached only 8 per cent light and 3 per cent moderate to vigorous levels of activity. Furthermore, teachers rarely prompted children to increase or decrease their physical activity.

There is clearly work to be done here to research the reasons why some staff themselves are physically inactive and what consequences this has for the children's development. Working with infants and young children can be physically demanding. Keeping fit and healthy will help those working in early childhood settings meet these demands each day (DH, 2011).

Physical activity guidelines for adults

The chief medical officers' guidelines (DH, 2011) recommend that adults be active on a daily basis, which should add up to at least 150 minutes over a week. This can be achieved by doing bouts of 10 minutes or more of moderate intensity activity, reaching 30 minutes on at least 5 days a week.

Vigorous intensity activity of 75 minutes spread across the week can deliver comparable benefits.

Adults are advised to take part in physical activity to improve muscle strength on at least two days a week. See Table 2.1 for examples of these different types of activity.

Table 2.1 *Examples of different types of activity*

Type of activity	Examples
Moderate intensity	Brisk walking, bike riding, dancing, swimming, active travel
Vigorous intensity	Running, playing sport, taking part in aerobic exercise, using cardiovascular gym equipment
Muscle strengthening	Weight training, working with resistance bands, carrying heavy loads, heavy gardening, push-ups, sit-ups

(DH, 2011)

Sedentary behaviour

Time spent being sedentary needs to be minimised for adults, too, such as sitting watching TV, using IT equipment, reading, listening to music or lying down for extended periods and using motorised transport (DH, 2011). The CMOs report that adults spend over seven hours per day being sedentary and this increases with age. Such behaviour is associated with being overweight, obesity, insulin resistance, type 2 diabetes, some cancers and cardiovascular and all-cause mortality (DH, 2011).

Conclusion

The findings outlined in this chapter about children's health are significant for those working in early education as they highlight the essential role of adults in intervening to increase children's levels of physical activity with positive consequences for their health. Details of how children can be physically active as provided by the CMOs and outlined in this chapter are clear and helpful for staff working in early childhood/primary education. Furthermore, parental support in helping young children to be physically active is vital. By working closely with parents and carers concerning the importance of physical activity for their children, early childhood settings can ensure an effective partnership develops in the interest of the children's health and well-being. Chapter 5 discusses the role of movement-play when developing partnerships with families.

Young children have increasing access to television and new technologies that demand more sedentary behaviour, yet nothing can replace the richness of experience for a child of playing outdoors in nature, feeling the rain or sun on their skin, laughing with their friends and racing across a field or playground. Professionals working in education and after school clubs, childminders, parents, grandparents – all need to be aware of the importance of reducing sedentary behaviours, increasing physical activity and establishing more active behaviours in their infants and young children (DH, 2011).

Particularly concerning is that, despite the attempt that policymakers have made to ensure that physical development plays an important role in young children's development, Archer and Siraj (2015) and Evangelou et al. (2009) revealed physical activity is not equally applied to all young children in all EYFS provisions.

Goddard Blythe (2005c: 175) argues that there is a failure 'to provide the space, the time, or the conditions in which free physical play can take place', the very type of activity the policymakers believe is critical to children's development. So, while there is an emphasis on the importance of physical activity and movement, in reality, early childhood settings are less enriched in terms of physical stimulation than they should be. Yet, authors such as Barsch (1968) described the young child as a terranaut. He argued that children must first learn to control their bodies on terra firma if they are to become secure in a gravity-based environment and make sense of the world around them.

Further research (Cosco et al., 2010; Trost et al., 2010) indicates that early childhood settings have a very strong influence on young children's physical activity levels, so they are significant environments in which to help young children obtain appropriate levels of daily physical movement (McWilliams et al., 2009).

Canadian research (Tucker et al., 2011) shows that early childhood providers need to better equip their classrooms and playrooms as well as outdoor spaces to improve physical activity levels for young children. Chapter 3 illustrates how early childhood environments can effectively promote children's physical development indoors and outdoors. Further descriptions and illustrations of the environment can be seen in Chapter 4, as well as the reasons for improving interactions between adults and children.

Brown et al. (2009) suggest that research should be undertaken to see if settings' policies incorporate physical activity. In one local authority we found that none of the early childhood centres had a written policy for physical development, despite this being a prime area of learning in the current EYFS in England. The final chapter in this book guides the reader in how to develop a policy on physical activity.

Further reading

British Heart Foundation (2012) 'Factors influencing physical activity in the early years: Fact sheet'. Available online at: www.bhfactive.org.uk/userfiles/Documents/factorsearlyyears.pdf

Department of Health (DH) (2011) 'Start Active, Stay Active: A report on physical activity from the four home countries' Chief Medical Officers' (Reference 16306). Available online at: www.gov.uk/government/uploads/system/uploads/attachment_data/file/216370/dh_128210.pdf

Hands, B.P. and Martin, M. (2003) 'Implementing a fundamental movement skill program in an early childhood setting: The children's perspectives'. *Australian Journal of Early Childhood*, 28 (4): 47–52. Available online at: http://researchonline.nd.edu.au/health_article/19

Panksepp, J. (1998) *Affective Neuroscience: The foundations of human and animal emotions*. New York: Oxford University Press.

3
Implementing a movement-play-based curriculum for children from birth to six years of age

Introduction

The task of introducing movement activities in a setting may appear quite daunting and planning and organisation may not work well at first or at all. Please do not give up – this situation is quite normal.

Training and experience over time as well as a will to learn from the children will undoubtedly equip all practitioners in this important work with them.

Please note that when we use the term 'practitioners', this includes early years educators, teachers and other qualified staff working with young children from birth to six years of age.

> ### Reflective practice
>
> Has a training session in movement-play been held at the setting for all the staff?
>
> Have the majority of members of staff at your setting received training in movement-play?
>
> What plans are there to ensure all new members of staff are trained in this area of the curriculum?

Babies

Adults often carry babies around the nursery. They will cuddle or dance with them, put them to bed, rock them to sleep, pick them up, put them down and turn them over. It is through taking part in these everyday movement conversations that adults and babies begin to form attachments.

At its simplest level, movement with babies will be based on the floor, where they will be lying on their backs or tummies or crawling, where adults join them, celebrating each tiny achievement in their development. The floor is their rehearsal space for perfecting these vital movement patterns. Babies begin with early reflex movements while lying on their backs or tummies, staying put in specific spaces where adults have placed them. In these places, babies enjoy the company of other babies and adults, communicating through moving their bodies, such as reaching out to be lifted up, kicking their legs and waving their arms in excitement, or through facial expressions, laughing and crying or babbling to express themselves.

Given time, babies will attempt to roll over, gradually lifting one hip and then the other until this rocking motion allows them to roll right over from their back to their front, and after much practice they will eventually reverse this movement. Babies begin to see their environment and the people around them from a different perspective the more mobile they become.

When babies are on their tummies, adults need to be down there with them, too, as they need company and someone to communicate with, make eye contact, smile and laugh with. Favourite toys placed just out of range will motivate babies to stretch their arms and wriggle their legs and eventually move by themselves to reach these. When babies begin to move on their tummies, they will move backwards at first and they may also go round and round on the same spot. Then, after a great deal of practice, they will move forwards. This is a baby's first self-determined movement, which deserves lots of praise and celebrating.

Some babies take to tummy time willingly and with enjoyment, while others are not so keen. When babies are reluctant tummy timers, it is best to find different ways for them to experience this movement pattern, such as gently rocking on a body ball or a rolling cushion or body painting.Babies enjoy lying on top of their father's or mother's body, coming face to face, ready for an interesting communication to take place between them.

Once confined to a specific space while laying on their backs or tummies, babies will eventually be able to move independently to explore their environment, transporting themselves from one place to another.

The one-year-old boy in the photograph has been persevering with tummy time and is now able to lift his upper body quite high, using his hands to push himself up. He can see all around him by turning his

head and eyes and will eventually be able to move his body to where he wants or needs to be. Notice that he has bare feet, which will help him, eventually, to propel himself forward.

Tummy time helps babies to create curves in their spines, strengthen muscles in their backs and necks and, as they hold their heads up, it will enable them to sit upright independently when their bodies are ready to do so. Sitting babies in equipment that holds them up before their bodies are ready interferes with the development of their spines and postural muscles and may affect their posture later on. If babies are not yet able to sit up independently, then they should not be placed in any equipment that holds them up unnaturally. If they are able to sit up independently, then they do not need equipment to hold them up. These pieces of equipment do nothing to trigger brain development as they render babies immobile and 'the baby will go into a neurologically neutral place and there is no time to waste in the first year of a baby's life being in neutral' (Lamont, 2011). Babies will show you when they can sit up by themselves.

Infants, however, who are sitting up unaided but rather passive, being disinclined to move independently, need to experience the feeling of movement, which can be achieved by holding them while dancing, spinning them gently in a rocker or laying them on material and gently pulling them along the floor. Infants at this stage of development are more likely to move independently when they have mastered tummy crawling. It is crucial that infants are put on to their tummies, even for short periods of time each day, to ensure that this vital movement pattern is not replaced by other ways of moving, such as bottom shuffling.

Tummy time lasts for a very short period when crucial neurological development takes place and must not be missed (Lamont, 2011). For further information about the link between early movement patterns and learning and development, see Chapter 1.

Infants who are ready to crawl on hands and knees will need a relatively clear floor space to move indoors or outdoors, so it is necessary to ensure that there are few obstacles impeding their progress. The world of the young infant is a sensory one – they need this to thrive and they enjoy exploring. This is no less so than when they play with gloop, paint, water and bubbles, wet sand, grass and mud, which provide important sensory experiences for them.

Crawling enables the feet and knees to line up with the hip sockets in preparation for walking and combines the use of touch and vision (Lamont, 2007a). Movement patterns that develop here will support posture, balance, coordination and spatial orientation and promote the cross-lateral pattern, which is when opposite sides of the body work together (Macintyre and McVitty, 2004).

In the photograph, the infant can be seen crawling outside on hands and knees, showing skill in moving in the contralateral pattern, which

means that when the right arm is forward, the left leg follows and when the left arm goes forward, the right leg will follow. She is laughing and looks very happy to be there. Her fingers are spreading out as she moves, too, which will help later with manipulating objects and, eventually, writing. Also, her eyes are tracking from left to right, which is a skill needed later for reading, and she is balancing with stability, her spine aligning from cranial to sacral regions, which will support her posture and muscle tone, ready for getting up on her feet and walking. These steps in her development cannot be fully achieved by sitting in a baby seat.

When ready to climb, the urge will be so strong that infants will climb wherever they possibly can, maybe into the sand tray or on top of a table, so make sure equipment is available to support them in this important step in their movement development. Infants unsteady on their feet will nevertheless determinedly rise on their two feet to walk and run. Infants are likely to be steadier when walking if they are barefoot as the connection to the floor can be felt much more keenly through the soles of their feet than through their shoes. Even at this stage of the infants' development, crawling should still be encouraged as so many benefits for their future development can still be derived from this early movement pattern.

The photograph shows that this infant has gained enough confidence in his balance and coordination while crawling down from the equipment

to feel able to reach out for ground level, hold his upper body up while bringing his legs down behind him. What an achievement!

Many challenging activities must be accessible indoors and outdoors for infants to engage in physically demanding play so that they can crawl through tunnels, spin in rocking cones, tumble in autumn leaves, play in the mud or snow or climb over soft play shapes on to a sofa, roll and tumble over cushions, climb stairs, come down a slide and swing.

Adults can safely provide babies with vigorous movement activities by swinging them in their arms or tossing them in the air, holding them upside down or gently rolling and tumbling with them. All these dynamic movements are really good for their vestibular system. For babies to experience joy and a willingness to persevere with movement activities, however, they need to feel safe with adults they can trust.

Observations of infants moving and their progress, interests and enjoyment will inform planning. Resources should be provided and organised appropriately for the needs of specific children or for a group of infants who are exploring similar movement patterns. The resources must be well presented and continually tidied and changed according to the infants' responses and needs. Observant adults will be noticing their levels of skill and refinement as the infants engage in movement activities each day. A well-planned environment will be safe for babies and allows sufficient space for them to move freely to explore both indoors and outdoors.

Two-year-olds

Two-year-olds walking without assistance are eager to explore their world with growing independence, though they are often still in need of frequent attention and contact with trusted adults around them. A balance gradually develops through negotiation between adults and individual toddlers regarding safety and closeness and the sheer delight in exploring and discovering their environment.

These young explorers enjoy walking, running, climbing and jumping as they learn about their own bodies and begin to view the world from a new perspective as they become more secure on their feet. When they first arrive at a nursery, it is movement-play activities that help them to settle into their new environment, watching or joining other children who they see having fun, but are doing serious work for their bodies and brains at the same time.

Two-year-olds are still learning to communicate verbally with each other and adults, but can also find movement conversations a playful communicative experience.

They are curious about their own bodies and like to talk about their body parts, such as hands, fingers, arms, elbows, legs, knees, ankles and toes, head, face, torso and other parts, too. They are also interested in what their bodies are capable of – how high they can jump, if they can roll all the way to the end of the mat or lie still like a 'sleeping bunny' and jump up again, as well as express themselves through dance.

Reflective practice

Do you *sometimes* include music with movement activities?

Do some children/adults use musical instruments as other children move and dance?

Two-year-olds are also still learning about safety and need to feel safe with adults nearby, supporting or moving with them. Initially, these young children feel safer when adults catch them as they jump from a height or hold a hand while balancing on logs, but, in time, after repeating this action time and again, children will gain the confidence and skill to be able to do this on their own.

All this learning takes time and practice and the adults (at home or in early childhood settings) need to provide the optimum environment to facilitate this. A wide range of equipment and resources will need to be accessible for two-year-olds to use when they need to, both indoors and outdoors, to enable them to achieve all that they need to.

Resources for indoors may include pillows, soft mats, large bean-bags, soft balls for tummy time; large body balls, Lycra material for rolling children inside, chiffon scarves for peek-a-boo; ribbon sticks or carnival sticks for dancing; plus material to hide under, cardboard boxes of various sizes, cotton-covered elastics of several sizes, tunnels and tumbling mats, and space to move how their imagination takes them for movement-play. An environment with access to these resources allows two-year-olds to experiment, be creative and explore their body potential through movement and dance on their own or with a partner or two or more.

More challenging activities indoors can be created with resources such as sofas and cushions for climbing up and rolling down or being held in the air by a trusted adult or adults allowing children to climb their legs and rolling right over or rolling over an adult's back as they crouch on the ground, crawling through an adult's legs, only to be lifted upside down and returned again to the floor. All these movements must be carried out with the consent and permission of the child.

Two-year-olds need a defined area indoors or a room specifically allocated for movement on a regular basis, whether this is daily or weekly. They should remove their shoes and socks when they want to join in with the activities and put them on again when they want to leave the area or room.

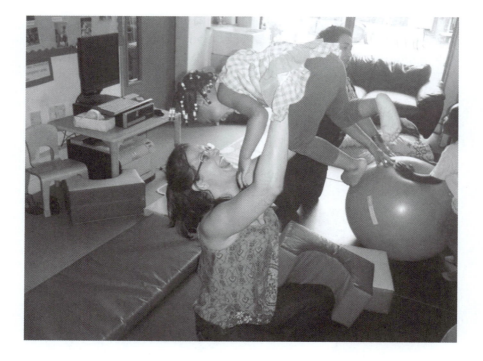

Movement activities should, ideally, be planned daily or weekly, indoors and outdoors, in response to children's interests, needs and schemas, and resources organised so that these are accessible to all the children.

Reflective practice

Is there sufficient space available in your setting for movement indoors when the weather is severe and children cannot go outside?

Has an early years educator been allocated responsibility for movement activities in the room or setting?

Who ensures that resources and space are ready for the children when they arrive in the morning or afternoon and that these remain looking attractive throughout the period of time they are accessible to the children?

Free-flow play allows two-year-olds to choose when they need to explore the outdoor or indoor environment, although all children need time outdoors to benefit from the more vigorous physical opportunities usually available to them there. They need to have access to indoor and outdoor play every day in line with the health recommendations outlined in Chapter 2. They need space to run, places to jump, balance, spin, roll, slide, swing, hang upside down, push and pull and carry relatively heavy items.

Equipment outdoors may include A-frames and ladders, balancing logs and planks, climbing walls, trees, slides, pulleys, sand, water, wheelbarrows, and uneven terrain with slopes and hills, as well as varied surfaces, including grass and mud.

As social beings, two-year-olds often seek company, with adults or their peers, and may climb trees with the help of an adult, ride a bike following a friend, pull another toddler along in a truck, dig mud, play imaginative games in a tree house, swing together on a frame or spin on spinning tops simultaneously with peers or adults.

They need space just to run, in bare feet or wearing shoes, on concrete or grass, across a playground or field, and feel the wind on their face, the sun on their bodies. Children need to feel the textures beneath their feet, when squelching their toes in mud or wet sand or splashing their feet in water, or feel the climbing holds on a climbing wall. How can they feel these sensations if they have their shoes and trainers on all the time?

All children need to be outdoors for their health and well-being, whatever the weather, wearing appropriate clothing and footwear in

the cold, wet and snow. They need time to put their coats on and pull on their wellington boots and practise these skills in their own time without being rushed, supporting self-regulation and well-being, while encouraged by a supportive adult, if needed.

Two-year-olds should be introduced to the equipment and its uses by watching adults and children using it, then trying it for themselves or with others, initially with help, then gradually with growing independence. The children will return again and again to the same movement experiences, practising emerging skills, discovering new ones and mastering others.

Movement patterns may take some children considerable time, through practice and repetition, to reach optimum development. The more opportunities each day or week children are provided with to engage in movement activities, therefore, the more likely they are to reach their full potential. That is why movement-play needs to be part of the curriculum planning each day, for all children, indoors and outdoors.

Two-year-olds will often play until they are exhausted, moving continually, but will willingly rest inside a box, swing a friend gently in a hammock or lay over a body ball as an adult rocks them to and fro. They will sometimes want to, or need to, slow down to have time to ponder the worm they find when digging in the earth, to smell a flower or lie down on the grass under a tree looking up at the sky.

Bringing children to stillness is essential for their well-being and development and should be included as part of their movement experiences.

Two-year-olds need access to sufficient floor space to move in a variety of ways, such as tummy crawling, crawling on hands and knees, rolling, spinning and rough and tumble.

The optimum area for young children to be physically active indoors is 50 per cent of the room space available. This should all be on the same level, so that it is accessible for, and inclusive of, all children, including children with disabilities. Ideally, free-flow play from indoors

to outdoors would also be possible, from when the children arrive to when they leave the setting to return home.

Some settings allocate the whole room to movement on a specific weekday, ensuring the inclusion of all children attending either morning or afternoon sessions. Other settings create an area for movement within the room on a specific day by pushing tables and chairs out of the way and this can then be used on a more regular basis. One setting decided, after movement-play training, to remove most of the tables and chairs permanently, devoting the majority of its large room to floor-based activities, which, the manager said, worked very well as children prefer lying on the floor to work than sitting at tables. In this way, children include more movements than before as they travel from one activity to another on their hands and knees or by sliding on their tummies.

Large mats provide a suitable surface for children to roll and tumble on, as well as a means of defining a movement area and a space to place resources such as boxes, Lycra, gold lamé material, chiffon scarves and rolling cushions. Also, leaving space around the mats allows toddlers to be pulled along while sitting inside a box placed on top of Lycra material, for example.

Resources need to be easily accessible to the children in the group. The range of activities provided, together with the organisation of the resources and the environment, ideally enable the children to spontaneously participate in movement activities alone or with their peers and adults.

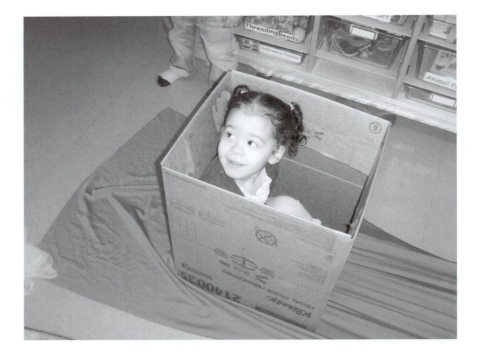

Three- to six-year-olds

Returning to early movement patterns is a must for preschool and early primary school children – or, indeed, anyone at any time of life (Lamont, 2007d). Tummy crawling and crawling on all fours should, therefore, be part of movement activities at every movement session because of the benefits they provide, including promoting strength, balance and coordination, which supports children's learning in more formal educational environments. Older children can be challenged by racing on their tummies or on all fours or being timed doing an obstacle course, moving over, under and through, throwing beanbags into hoops or balls into a bucket while crawling on all fours, blowing table tennis balls through a straw from one end of the hall to the other while on their tummies, designing and building a piece of equipment that they can tummy crawl along, up and down and so on. It is important that all the movement patterns are covered and children's interests, schemas and needs are planned for, too.

Feeling textures with bare feet is also important for all children and there are numerous ways in which this can be carried out indoors and outdoors, including holding a child while they kick a large body ball

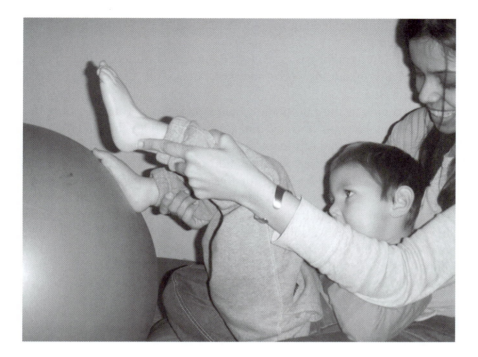

or by their rolling in a tunnel

or by just running, feeling the sensations of the ground through the soles of their feet.

Some children might have developed enough confidence and competence to hang upside down on monkey bars or an A-frame or climb a climbing wall.

The two girls in the photograph below are competently climbing the wall, holding on with tenacity and pushing up with their feet on the climbing holds. They both leapt on to the wall and reached the top in seconds! Can you see the determination on the face of the girl on the right? Her left hand is reaching for the next climbing hold, but hasn't quite got there, so she is also holding on with just one hand at the precise moment the photograph was taken. If you look closely, you will be able to see that she is also looking up for the next hold where her left hand will go. Notice, too, that she doesn't need to look at her hand to know where it is while she is reaching up as her proprioceptive system has developed sufficiently for this to be unnecessary. Instead, she can keep her eyes on the next climbing hold.

CASE STUDY

A child at a children's centre climbed right to the top of the climbing wall for the very first time and she was so pleased with herself that she told the practitioner she would wait there until her mum came to collect her at home time so she could see she had reached the top. Her mother wasn't due to arrive for at least another half an hour or so and the practitioner took the time to patiently persuade her to come down, convincing her that she would be able to do it again when her mum came – which she did! What a sense of achievement and pride for this child. This was celebrated by both the staff and parent.

The photograph below shows a preschooler hanging from the ladder of an A-frame as she confidently and expertly turns her body round to reposition herself so that she is holding on to the bar of the ladder with one hand, turning her legs and feet round in order that she could reach for the ground with her other hand. This action demands

strength in both hands and arms, which are supporting her body while she is upside down, helping her to remain stable, as she brings her whole body round in a coordinated movement from one shape into another. This action stimulates both the vestibular and proprioceptive systems.

The two girls in the following photograph enjoyed hanging from the monkey bars, swinging and turning upside down. As children move in this way, they stimulate the proprioceptive system, which enables them to know where their limbs are without having to look at them. This is important when doing a complicated movement, such as this, which requires precise coordination.

Three- to six-year-olds need lots of challenging activities, such as building dens, digging the earth to plant trees, plants, bulbs, herbs and vegetables to cook and eat, and, in so doing, will learn about their environment. They may want to dig the earth to find worms, identifying the particular species living in their garden, using the Internet or reference books to find out what they feed on, their life span, how long they grow, what benefits they bring to the soil and how to care for them. Resources such as wheelbarrows, reclaimed bricks and wet sand provide stimulating and problemsolving opportunities for children of this age to build walls or other structures related to their interests or the projects the setting is focusing on. Alternatively, children may choose to transport heavy items, such as water to add to sand or to water plants, or use hollow wooden blocks for constructing a building they have been designing. These activities involve lots of heavy lifting and transporting, which stimulates the proprioceptive system and may also appeal to children who are exploring the transporting schema.

Children can be involved in the planning of daily movement activities. Staff should be talking to them about what they would like to do or resources they would like to use. This will encourage the children to be able to express their movement needs using vocabulary and language that are relevant and in context and contribute towards the selection of resources and their organisation, as well as problemsolving.

What resources are you providing in your setting for children to build dens?

Designing, building and using an obstacle course, for example, involves planning, experimenting, problemsolving and using lots of language for movement, including verbs and prepositions, such as when they '*climb up* a ladder, *crawl through* a tunnel, *slide down* a slide, *tummy crawl under* a plank, *roll along* the mats, *spin inside* the spinning cone and *hang upside down on* the frame'. They will need to decide where to place pieces of equipment, whether the tunnel will go '*on* top of a frame or *between* the ladder and slide, if the mats will be placed *beside* the slide as well as *in front of* the spinning cone and whether the frame will be at the beginning or end of the course'. Obstacle courses provide opportunities for children to adjust their balance and coordination as they negotiate equipment at various heights from the ground up.

Maude (2008: 251) suggests that children become increasingly 'physically literate' through movement experiences in their early years. She argues that we should use accurate and applicable vocabulary with children, extending their language through expressive movement activities, using words such as twirl, crouch, glide, hover, leap, settle, expand, collapse, push, pull, turn, flutter, sway, roll (Maude, 2010). Children need to experience a varied and worthwhile movement vocabulary in order to broaden their physical literacy. To achieve this, they need a relevant and effective movement curriculum that cultivates skilful, articulate and creative movement in children and the role of the educator is central to this (Maude, 2008).

Preschool children and children in their early primary years may enjoy designing and building their own balancing equipment and deciding which pieces of equipment they would like to use. Balance is an important movement skill for young children and developing it is crucial to their future life.

Children love to jump up and down or jump from a great height and may spontaneously build themselves a platform to jump off from at a height that challenges them and suits their needs. Such activities stimulate the vestibular system, which will support the development of balance.

The following photograph shows a child rolling down a hill, which this nursery built specifically for toddlers and preschool children to roll down, climb up and down, to carry things up and push things down, thus stimulating their balance system.

If children are able to balance, then they will be able to control their bodies in movement and stillness and, therefore, be more capable of sitting still when needed and concentrating on more sedentary tasks, such as reading, listening to stories and writing.

Goddard Blythe (2014) is concerned about the number of children starting school who are unable to sit still or stand up straight or hold a pencil – all indicative of poor physical development and likely to influence progress and achievement in various areas of learning, including literacy and numeracy. If children experience difficulty sitting still or have poor posture and/or coordination, this means that they need to be given more movement activities.

The mini spinners shown in the photograph below are suitable for stimulating the vestibular systems of children aged two to six. If, however, observations reveal that the difficulties preventing a child from progressing are persisting, then it is important to seek advice from a movement specialist or an occupational therapist or the Institute for Neuro-Physiological Psychology (INPP).

Children in preschool and primary school also need to come to quietness and stillness. Some settings have quiet spaces for children, such as a tepee, den, hammocks, or simply a large cardboard box. A number of settings that have received training in movement-play are bringing children to stillness at the end of a movement session indoors or when they can see the children need to be still and quiet, such as when the weather is particularly warm outside and they are getting quite hot and bothered. One group of preschool children were asked to lie still outside on the ground on a warm day and watch the clouds drift by, listening to the sounds they could hear around them. They all lay quietly for some time and, after a while, one child sat up quite suddenly, exclaiming that she could hear the birds singing!

This tepee was painted by parents, children and staff – a place for children to be on their own or share with a friend or two. Sometimes children have their snacktime or storytime inside the tepee.

You can see from the first photograph on page 64 that there is limited space in this room to allocate to movement, but the staff ensure at least once a week they dedicate this ardance and do things their bodies need to do. To enhance safety, soft mats have been placed in front of the shelving around this space. This setting allows the childea to resources that encourage children to roll, rough and tumble, jump, ren to freely move from indoors to outdoors and vice versa, all day, whatever the weather.

The nursery in the bottom photograph also always saves its large cardboard boxes for a variety of activities children can undertake indoors or outdoors. These are an invaluable, free resource for all preschool and reception-age children.

Reflective practice

Is the outdoor area open from the time the children enter the room in the morning until home time, excluding lunchtime and sleep time for the younger children?

If you have no outdoor space, do you take the children out every day to a local park to use playground equipment or a play area or field where the children can run and roll around, sing and dance?

Assessing the setting in terms of space and resources, adults engaging in movement with the children and planning for movement from observations can be carried out by using the movement-play scale provided in Chapter 4.

Adults engaging in movement with the children

In an environment in which infants, two-year-olds, preschool and early primary school-age children can move freely to express themselves through movement, adults provide the appropriate environmental context for the children's developmental level. In this context staff are willing to join children on the floor as they move, following their lead and responding to their innovative ways of moving. Those children who do not appear confident about joining in movement activities or using specific materials and equipment may need prompting or support to do so. Adults recognise when children are capable of engaging in specific physical activities alone or when they need help through their ongoing observations of the children. Indeed, movement-play is an inclusive practice and staff always need to ensure that all children, able and with disabilities, are included.

Movement needs to be acknowledged, nurtured and celebrated by staff as a key aspect of children's development. Staff can understand and value movement by watching children move with attention and support them in the creative ways in which they choose to move. Children's interests and schemas can be identified and extended through providing appropriate resources or support.

Working with parents

Staff and parents must share information about the physical activities children enjoy at the nursery or primary school and at home indoors and outdoors. Settings we have worked with have collected information from parents about activities their children do outside of the sessions, using 'Wow!' cards to record when parents are delighted by something their children have done at home or forms such as those shown in Chapter 5.

The completed forms we saw included photographs showing the types of physical activities the children engaged in with their parents when at home or away. The setting set up a display using these photographs that had been sent in by parents, together with those of children being physically active at the setting, illustrating the range of activities they were engaging in. Meetings with parents were then held to show a film about children moving, learning and growing (see Chapter 5 for more details) and talk about how physical development through movement-play supports their children's health, well-being, learning and overall development.

A leaflet about movement-play produced for parents was given to them and the film was also loaned to them. In these ways, opportunities can be offered to parents to develop a mutual understanding and appreciation of how their children move, grow and learn.

> ### Reflective practice
>
> Have you held a parents meeting about movement-play for either mothers or fathers or both?

Planning for movement from observations of the children

Well-trained and knowledgeable staff regularly observe children's responses to movement activities indoors and outdoors and plan for their interests, schemas and needs. Movement activities are planned for specific children in response to observations that are written into the daily and weekly plans.

> ### Reflective practice
>
> Do you monitor how physically active individual children are and what movements they engage in throughout a day or over a week?

Observations might reveal that one child craves activities such as spinning around over and over again until he or she falls down or spinning on the floor on his or her bottom or in a spinning cone. This may indicate a schema, otherwise known as a repeated pattern of behaviour, which may also be reflected in the child's drawings or paintings showing lots of circular marks, for example, or the making of repeated circular actions, such as moving a train round and round a track.

> **Reflective practice**
>
> Are movement activities written into your planning each week?
>
> How often do you plan for movement activities for the whole group, small groups and individual children?

Assessments

Achievements will be observed and significant moments or milestones recorded for all infants, toddlers, preschool and early primary school-age children by the early years educator or teacher, which may be placed in the child's learning journey or portfolio. Children's learning journeys or portfolios will include their progress in movement patterns over time, with photos and written observations.

Staff reflect on parents' observations of their children at home and use this information in each child's portfolio and planning. If other professionals, such as occupational therapists, are working with a child. then relevant information from their assessments should also be included in the daily or weekly plans.

A summative assessment of children's progress in physical development is usually written at the end of each term or at the end of the year. The EYFS requires early years practitioners to review children's progress and share a summary with parents in the prime curriculum areas between the ages of 24 and 36 months.

Conclusion

Early childhood settings are in a key position to significantly contribute towards children's future health, learning and development through the quality of the environment they provide and the adults' engagement with the children. The setting's policy on physical development will support the effective implementation of the plans for this crucial area of learning for children from birth to six years of age. Chapter 6 provides extensive information on how to draw up a physical development policy, starting with practice.

Further reading

Athey, C. (2007) *Extending Thought in Young Children: A parent–teacher partnership* (Second Edition). London: Paul Chapman.

Davies, M. (2003) *Movement and Dance in Early Childhood (0–8 years)* (Second Edition). London: Sage.

Le Voguer, M. and Pasch, J. (2014) 'Physical well-being: Autonomy, exploration, and risk taking'. In J. Manning-Morton (ed.), *Exploring Well-being in the Early Years*. Maidenhead: Open University Press.

Macintyre, C. and McVitty, K. (2004) *Movement and Learning in the Early Years: Supporting dyspraxia and other difficulties*. London: Sage.

Maude, P. (2008) 'How do I do this better?: From movement development into physical literacy'. In D. Whitebread and P. Coltmman (eds), *Teaching and Learning in the Early Years* (Third Edition). Abingdon: Routledge.

Mountstephen, M. (2011) *How to Detect Developmental Delay and What to do Next: Practical interventions for home and school*. London: Jessica Kingsley.

4
Improving the quality of movement-play: a small-scale study

Introduction

Previous chapters have carefully presented reasons why movement is essential for young children, in terms of their health, well-being, brain development and learning, and movement activities to help achieve these benefits have been described. The value of physical development for young children has been recognised by successive governments in England. The latest early years curriculum guidance has identified physical development as one of three prime areas of learning for young children.

There is a relationship between the quality of the environment and outcomes for children. Sylva et al. (2004), in their study, the Effective Provision of Pre-school Education (EPPE), found that high-quality early childhood settings have a significant impact on outcomes for children. In their examination of the characteristics of an effective setting, Sylva et al. (2004) used mixed research methods, including the Early Childhood Environment Rating Scales (ECERS-R) (Revised) and ECERS-E (Extension).

At the time of our study, there was, to our knowledge, no straightforward means of assessing the quality of movement-play. We therefore developed a movement-play scale (MPS) modelled on the ECERS-E prior to carrying out the study. For a reader who has not yet been introduced to these early childhood rating scales, they are used widely internationally to assess and improve quality in a number of areas of provision and practice. The movement-play scale we devised will be described fully later in this chapter and is included to use for staff development and self-assessment.

Children can be supported in the early childhood context in terms of how environments are organised, what resources are provided and child–adult and child–child interactions in areas related to children's interests. The crucial question relates to quality and how that is assessed.

In addition to the movement-play scale, interviews and observations were carried out prior to commencing the study and again at the end to give as complete a picture as possible.

This chapter will describe the study, which was carried out in an inner-city borough of London in the UK by the authors. It will also discuss the implementation of movement-play in these early childhood settings.

This is the first study to assess the quality of the environment and practice in relation to movement-play. Our findings reveal that an intervention in the form of staff training, advice and support resulted in important improvements in the role of the adults, influencing the quality and range of the children's movement experiences. This result, together with data gathered from interviews with managers and staff, will be of interest to those responsible for making crucial decisions about policy and practice in early childhood settings and schools.

The movement-play scale is currently being employed in a number of early childhood settings in England and beyond. During 2013, the scale was administered in a pilot study and followed up by a main study in 2014–2015 in 600 preschool and kindergarten classrooms in Greece, as part of research evaluating physical activity in early childhood education.

A small-scale study

As noted above, this was a small-scale study undertaken in four early childhood settings in an inner-city borough of London in order to find out whether or not an intervention resulted in improved movement experiences for young children.

The movement-play scale devised was used to assess the quality of movement-play before and after the training intervention. The intervention comprised one day of movement-play training, followed by four sessions of follow-up support and advice at the two intervention settings.

The other two settings did not receive an intervention for the purposes of comparison. In order that staff in the comparison settings felt comfortable with their involvement and so the research would be ethical, training was offered to them on a date after the completion of the study.

This study has wider implications, too – for parents, policymakers and others – with regard to physical development in the early years curriculum and children's 'school readiness'.

Assessing quality

Research has shown that high-quality care is associated with improved developmental outcomes for children and, conversely, lower-quality care is associated with poorer outcomes (Belsky, 2001; Peisner-Feinberg et al., 2000; Sylva et al., 2006a). Some go so far as to say that children from disadvantaged backgrounds are considered to be the most affected by the quality of care (McCartney et al., 2007).

Clearly the quality of care at early childhood settings makes a difference to children. Early childhood rating scales, such as the ECERS-R, ECERS-E and ITERS-R, have been used widely to assess and measure quality in a number of areas of provision and practice. The importance of the rating scales lies in the findings of many studies, which have shown that they can predict children's development (Mathers et al., 2007). In the context of our small-scale study, this is important because children's engagement in movement-play affects their learning and development.

The ECERS-E was specifically developed for use in Sylva et al.'s (2004) longitudinal research, the Effective Provision of Pre-school Education in the UK (EPPE). The original EPPE study was the first major study in the UK to focus specifically on the effectiveness of early childhood education. The ECERS-R and ECERS-E were employed in this valuable piece of research. The ECERS-E was used specifically for assessing curricular aspects of quality, including pedagogy, thus supplementing the broad and balanced focus of the ECERS-R. When compared, the ECERS-R is more sensitive to quality related to children's social-behavioural development, while the ECERS-E is more sensitive to children's cognitive progress and their academic skills (Sylva et al., 2006). The EPPE study investigated children's intellectual and social/behavioural development, focusing on preschool influences. Thus, quality may be considered in terms of environments, curricula and pedagogy.

The ECERS-E is a particularly valuable extension for institutional self-assessment and improving pedagogy and the curriculum in early childhood settings. Its subscales contain items covering four specific aspects of learning and development: literacy, mathematics, science and the environment and diversity. The ECERS-E has been used by a number of local authorities as one way to assess quality in their provision so that each child's learning and development can thrive.

The focus of our study was to assess quality in relation to the environment and pedagogy by creating and using the movement-play scale. The movement-play items, modelled on the ECERS-E, were an attempt to develop a measure that can provide an informed, yet objective assessment of quality in the area of movement-play for young children.

The pilot study

The scale was piloted specifically for the purpose of this study in order to trial the items to assess how well they worked and how reliable they were. From this, it was ascertained what adaptations needed to be made so that it could be used in the study in the four settings.

A total of eight settings participated in the pilot study, including one children's centre, five private nurseries, one specialist nursery for children with speech, language and hearing problems and one nursery class in a maintained school. A movement practitioner working in a borough of London also trialed the scale. In total, 12 practitioners agreed to trial the scale within their 8 settings. The age ranges of the children attending these settings varied, but, overall, they included babies, toddlers and preschool children.

The findings indicated that 80 per cent of the participants found all the items 'easy' to use and 'useful' for measuring quality at their settings. One participant commented that 'the layout of this scale is progressive' and 'it had been useful in guiding improvement in their environment and practice'. Participants who responded negatively had not used the ECERS before, which may have accounted for their difficulty in administering the scale, though they were familiar with movement-play. Further remarks indicated that it provided a 'common language' for professionals to use, with the aim of improving movement experiences for children.

Amendments were subsequently made to the scale so that it was ready to use in the study.

The movement-play scale (MPS)

The development of the MPS was an important part of the process of improving quality in the area of physical development within early childhood settings. By addressing physical development through movement-play, we were responding to the evidence discussed in the previous chapters that movement activities influence children's health, well-being and brain development. In this way, overall quality in a setting could be further enhanced through strengthening its curriculum.

Settings were selected by the authors on the basis of their similarity to each other in terms of their size and the age groups of the children attending in order to be able carry out a useful comparative analysis. All the settings considered for selection therefore included children aged from four months to five years. The selection process involved early years advisory teachers with responsibility for supporting the selected settings, who then approached the managers for their consent to be involved in the study. All the settings agreed which role would suit them best – that is, as either an intervention or comparison setting.

It was not possible in this small-scale study to find completely similar groups prior to the intervention and, therefore, settings were selected on a 'best fit' basis. Accordingly, all four of the settings selected were in the private sector, with rooms for babies, toddlers and preschool children. The numbers of children in each setting ranged from 6 to 9 babies; 12 to 16 toddlers; and 16 to 24 preschool children.

The MPS consists of three items:

Item 1: Space and resources
Item 2: Adults engaging in movement with the children
Item 3: Planning for movement-play from observations of the children

Descriptions of each of the three items can be found below.

All three items rate quality within a range starting from inadequate, to minimal, to good, then through to excellent. Each item includes a number of indicators to use to identify progression. All three items are accompanied by extensive notes for clarification that enable users to accurately interpret the indicators. If the scale is being used for research, training is required for its use, but otherwise, for self-assessment and professional development, it can be discussed and used by staff without training.

Item 1: Space and resources

This item assesses quality in terms of the space accessible indoors for children to move in a variety of ways. This would be affected by whether tables and chairs dominate the room or whether the floor is freely accessible for floor-based activities to take place. Indicators in this item also address the accessibility of outdoor space, resources and activities.

Notes for clarification of this item are comprehensive, detailing safety, measurement of space and definitions of terms in the indicators. It lists resources for each age group, defines challenging activities and outlines a range of activities needed for babies, toddlers and nursery-age children.

Questions are also listed in the notes for clarification in order to ascertain the use of resources and availability of space when the weather is bad.

Item 2: Adults engaging in movement with the children

The indicators in this item assess the level of the members of staff's engagement with the children in movement activities, including vigorous activities. They ascertain whether they have been trained and if they are reading to extend their knowledge and understanding.

This item expects staff to be engaging parents by sharing information, knowledge and understanding. It also requires the setting to invite external movement specialists to come in or for the members of staff to take children to see acrobatic or dance performances.

The notes for clarification define terms such as 'sometimes' and 'regularly', as well as 'vigorous activities'. Ideas for sharing with parents are listed, as well as nurturing and celebrating movement as a key aspect of the children's development.

Questions in the notes for clarification seek to ascertain the frequency of movement activities carried out with children, whether or not music is included and if meetings with parents have taken place.

Item 3: Planning for movement-play from observations of the children

Indicators assess if observations and planning are undertaken at all, through to whether or not members of staff are observing and planning movement activities for individual children. Indicators in this item also identify if parents and professionals, such as occupational therapists, are also contributing to observations and planning.

Notes for clarification define terms such as 'some' and 'regularly', with questions to clarify the levels of staff training, details of written planning and frequency of planning for the whole group, small groups and individual children.

The MPS shows how progress can be made across the three items. It is anticipated that this scale will help members of staff to consider their environment, clarify their pedagogical aims and respond appropriately to children's developmental needs and interests. Additionally, the scale is a prompt for them to bring together knowledge about the children from their time at the setting and from the parents' and/or carers' knowledge of the children at home. See Table 4.1 on page 76 for details of the MPS, notes for clarification, questions and other details.

Table 4.1 Movement-play scale (MPS) with notes for clarification and questions

Movement-play scale

Item 1: Space and resources

Inadequate 1	2	Minimal 3	4	Good 5	6	Excellent 7
1.1 Little opportunity for movement-play experiences for children.		3.1 Children have access to some floor space for movement indoors. (a)		5.1 Sufficient floor space is available indoors for children to move in a variety of ways, such as tummy time, crawling, rolling, spinning and rough and tumble. (d)		7.1 The range of activities provided together with the organisation of the resources and environment enable children to spontaneously participate in movement activities alone or with their peers and adults. (f)
1.2 Little space for children to move.		3.2 Some resources are provided that encourage children to move in a variety of ways. (b)		5.2 Space and resources are easily accessible for children in the group (for example, they are on the same level and in the room; no barriers for children with disabilities).		7.2 There is a wide range of equipment and resources easily accessible for children to use when they want to or need them, indoors and outdoors. (g)
1.3 Routines dominate the day.		3.3 Children have access each day to movement outdoors. (c)		5.3 Many challenging activities must be accessible outdoors for children to engage in physically demanding play. (e)		
(It is important to also read the notes for clarification and questions opposite)						

* 'Children' includes babies, toddlers, nursery and reception age children

Carol Archer, Early Years Advisory Teachers

(April 2012)

Notes for clarification

Movement-play scale, Item 1: Space and resources

Please note: Safety in terms of appropriateness and condition of space and equipment applies to all the points below. Mats and cushioning surfaces must be available for free fall and rough and tumble activities indoors and outdoors. Equipment in all areas must be safe so that major causes of serious injury are minimised. Adults must join children in their play or be nearby to ensure babies and children are safe. Any activities with babies and children must be carried out with their consent.

'Movement-play activities' include babies being on their backs and tummies, pushing up off the floor with their hands while on their tummies, rolling over, crawling and pulling themselves up. Later on, children will climb, jump, balance, swing, run, spin until they fall over, hang upside down skip, push and pull heavy items, rough and tumble.

(a) 'Some floor space' means approximately 25 per cent of the floor space in the room indoors is available for movement indoors.

(b) 'Some resources' means that there are at least three different types of resources accessible to children from the following lists:

- **for babies:** pillows and soft mats in defined area, small soft balls, large body balls, Lycra, chiffon scarves, tunnel, tumbling mats, carnival sticks, shallow spinning cone, baby gym with slide, stairs and tunnels. For babies and children who seem immobile or reluctant to engage in movement activities, adults will need to provide daily opportunities for tummy time.

- **for pre-school and reception age children:** cardboard boxes, space blanket, tubes, pillows, small soft balls, large body balls, Lycra, large cotton-covered elastic, carnival sticks, ribbon sticks, chiffon scarves, tunnels, spinning cone, balancing equipment, nursery gym with slide, stairs and tunnel and tumbling mats.

(c) 'Access ... to movement outdoors' means at least one hour each day in a setting open for four hours a day and proportionally more for settings open for longer hours.

(d) 'Sufficient floor space' means that at least 50 per cent of the floor space in the room indoors is available for movement activities.

(e) 'Many challenging activities' means that more than three of the following types of equipment are also accessible for at least half the children to use at once from the following:

- **for babies:** floor space for babies to be on their backs and tummies, tunnels to crawl through, shallow spinning cone, soft play shapes to climb and jump off, Lycra material for rocking babies in, baby gym with stairs, slide and tunnel (adults can also swing babies in their arms, hold babies upside down).

- **for pre-school and reception age children:** spinning cone, slide, swing, A-frames and ladders, trampoline, monkey bars, climbing walls, climbing frames, trees to climb, equipment to jump off, equipment for balancing, swinging, tug of war, climbing over and under adult bodies, rough and tumble and wheelbarrows and bricks.

- Stationary and portable equipment need to meet this standard. To give credit, these types of equipment need to be accessible for a substantial portion of the day.

(f) 'The range of activities' means that there are opportunities for babies and children to take part in five or more of the activities listed below (and space is available) so that:

- **babies:** can be on their backs and tummies on the floor and can roll, crawl, climb, slide, spin, jump, hang upside down, push and pull

- **pre-school and reception age children:** can run, jump, spin, roll, crawl, be on their tummies, hang, slide, balance, climb, skip, swing, rough and tumble and push and pull or carry heavy items.

(g) 'A wide range of equipment and resources' would include sufficient resources for children to be able to engage in the range of activities described above.

Questions

1. How often do children use the resources available to them?
2. Is there space available for movement indoors when the weather is bad?

Movement-play scale

Item 2: Adults engaging in movement with the children

Inadequate 1	2	Minimal 3	4	Good 5	6	Excellent 7
1.1 Staff rarely move with the children. *(It is important to read the notes for clarification and questions opposite)*		3.1 Children are sometimes joined by staff in their movement-play indoors. *(a)* 3.2 Staff encourage children to move in a variety of ways indoors and outdoors. 3.3 At least one member of staff has attended movement-play training.		5.1 Staff join in children's movement following their lead and responding to children's innovative ways of using equipment regularly. *(b)* Staff willing to join children on the floor in their movement activities. Staff prompt children to move who seem to be immobile. Staff ensure that children with disabilities are included. 5.2 Children engage in a variety of movement activities, including vigorous activities *(c)*, on their own or with peers, inside and outside. 5.3 Staff share information about movement-play with parents. *(d)* 5.4 Movement is acknowledged by adults, nurtured and celebrated as a key aspect of children's development. *(e)* 5.5 The majority of members of staff have attended training and workshops/forums. They increase their knowledge and understanding about movement-play through reading.		7.1 Children are encouraged to freely express themselves through movement. Members of staff understand and value body movement by watching with attention and supporting the creative ways children move. 7.2 Activities that extend children's interest in movement are offered at least once a year, such as visits from a movement specialist, or trained yoga teachers working with children, or there are dance performances at the setting, or visits to theatres to see acrobatic or dance performances. 7.3 Opportunities are offered to parents to develop a mutual understanding and appreciation of children moving, growing and learning. *(f)* 7.4 Staff extend their knowledge and understanding through additional reading and attending further courses.

* 'Children' includes babies, toddlers, nursery and reception age children

Carol Archer, Early Years Advisory Teachers

(April 2012)

Notes for clarification

Movement-play scale, Item 2: Adults engaging in movement with the children

(a) 'Sometimes' means at least once a week.

(b) 'Regularly' means approximately three to five times a week.

(c) 'Vigorous activities' include:

- **for babies:** being tossed in the air, swinging babies in your arms, tummy time, crawling, rolling, climbing, holding babies upside down.
- **for pre-school and reception age children:** hanging from A-frames or monkey bars, spinning and falling, pulling, pushing and carrying heavy things, tug of war, climbing, jumping and running.

(d) For example, at least two of the following are shared with parents and carers: movement play leaflet for parents; meeting with parents and carers to discuss movement play and the benefits for their children; the DVD *Moving, Learning and Growing* to be shown at a parents meeting; displays and/or a portfolio of children engaged in movement activities, explaining the benefits.

(e) This includes, for example, joining children in their movement, displaying photos of children's engagement in movement activities, making booklets with children about their movement activities.

(f) Parents are offered the DVD to take home on loan; parents take home a copy of the movement-play leaflet for parents, parents are loaned resources to take home to use with their child or children in movement activities, the ways their child or children like to move at home and at the setting are discussed with parents with a view to offering opportunities to develop their interests and schemas.

Questions

1. How often do you do movement activities with the children?
2. Do you use music with movement activities? Do some children and adults use musical instruments as other children move and dance?
3. Have you held a parents meeting about movement-play for either mothers or fathers or other carers or all?

Movement-play scale

Item 3: Planning for movement-play from observations of the children

Inadequate 1	2	Minimal 3	4	Good 5	6	Excellent 7
1.1 No observations of children's movement activities.		3.1 Staff make some observations of children's engagement in movement activities. *(a)*		5.1 Staff regularly observe children's specific responses to movement activities indoors and outdoors. They observe and respond to the needs of individual babies and children. *(c)*		7.1 Trained and knowledgeable staff incorporate into their planning specific movement activities identified from observations indoors and outdoors of individual children's interests and needs.
1.2 No written planning undertaken, which includes movement activities.		3.2 Observations are kept in children's portfolios and sometimes used in planning. *(b)*		5.2 Plans are written in response to observations made of children's interests and need for specific movement activities.		7.2 Movement activities are designed for specific children's needs, which are written into weekly plans.
(It is important to read the notes for clarification and questions opposite)				5.3 Parents and practitioners share observations of children engaging in movement activities at home and at the setting.		7.3 Parents' observations are included in planning and observational assessment. Other professionals, such as occupational therapists, working with individual children, contribute to planning.
				5.4 Children's portfolios include their progress in movement-play with photos and/or written observations.		

* 'Children' includes babies, toddlers, nursery and reception age children

Carol Archer, Early Years Advisory Teachers

(April 2012)

Notes of clarification

Movement-play scale, Item 3: Planning for movement-play from observations of the children

(a) 'Some' means about once a month for at least one child.
(b) 'Sometimes' means at least once a week and written on the planning sheet.
(c) 'Regularly' means once a fortnight for babies and once a month for pre-school and reception age children, with a written record in the children's portfolios and on the planning sheets.

Questions

1. How many members of staff have attended training in movement-play?
2. Are movement activities written into your planning each week?
3. How often do you plan for movement activities for the whole group, small groups and individual children?

It is permissible to photocopy the MPS. Please contact the authors if you have any results to pass on or comments to make on its use. We would be delighted to hear from you.

The intervention for the study

Research (Siraj-Blatchford et al., 2002) shows that practitioner knowledge and understanding of any particular curriculum being addressed are vital. Members of staff in early childhood provison need to have a 'good grasp' of 'pedagogical content knowledge' in order to be effective educators of young children (Sylva et al., 2004: 38). Furthermore, Evangelou et al. (2009: 5), remind us that, 'Enhancing children's development is skilful work and practitioners need training and support to do it well'. An important aspect of this study, therefore, was the intervention, which included training whole teams of staff, including managers and deputies, in movement-play. Further consideration was given to the settings' effective implementation of the training in order to enhance quality. To that end, members of staff were given four follow-up sessions of support and advice at each of the intervention settings.

The movement-play training involved practical work for all participants, who were required to physically move through significant movement patterns typical of most infants, starting from a foetal position, followed by movement on their backs and tummies, then crawling on all fours, spinning, rolling, then ending with pushing and pulling. As each movement pattern was explored practically, the benefits to children's development were explained.

One session involved talking about children attending the setting whose development was of concern and advising staff on specific and/ or enhanced movement activities to support them. Members of staff reorganised their rooms or discussed strategies for implementing ideas, organising or listing the resources needed, and considered planning.

Advice and support

The four sessions of support and advice with the intervention settings were undertaken after the training. They involved the use of 'unstructured interviews' (Roberts-Holmes, 2011: 5), consisting of what Siraj-Blatchford (2010: 225) describes as 'conversations with a purpose'. This provided respondents with the maximum amount of freedom in determining their responses. In this way, the researchers' role was to act as a 'conversation facilitator' and therefore, to an extent, the sessions were 'led by the interviewees' responses' (Roberts-Holmes, 2011: 5). This was an important approach as it elicited as much information as possible, which helped the study to achieve greater validity and understanding of how the researcher could best support and advise the practitioners.

Data collection

The MPS was administered at the first intervention setting and the comparison setting in the same week. The same process was followed with the second intervention and comparison settings a month later. Observations were carried out at each nursery when the scale was used in all rooms covering all age groups – that is, babies, toddlers and pre-school children before and after the intervention.

After the training, the intervention settings agreed on dates for four sessions of follow-up support and advice. At each of the sessions, the room leaders and setting managers were informally interviewed to gather information in order to assess how the implementation was proceeding.

At the end of the four-week period, the MPS was administered again in each of the rooms at the intervention and comparison settings. Both pre- and post-assessments were administered in all four settings to enable a comparative analysis to be made.

Meetings were held to provide feedback to all the staff teams at the intervention settings.

Validity and reliability

The use of the MPS has been limited to a small pilot study and its application to this small-scale study. We accept that a larger-scale research study and extensive field studies would be needed to demonstrate that the qualities measured by this scale have validity and test the reliability of the indicators in terms of their having some predictive value for children's development. This would require some assessment of children's physical development, too.

Changes in practice observed by researchers over the period of the study may have been unrelated to the intervention. An honest attempt was made, however, to ensure that the intervention was measured accurately. Further data were obtained from informal conversations in order to build a fuller and more accurate picture of the changes made to practice.

Data were collected after the scale was administered at each nursery and the results compiled into tables and graphs.

The results

The MPS enabled data to be gathered. Quantitative data provided evidence concerning the quality of the spaces and resources in the settings, the adults' engagement in movement with the children and the level of planning for movement resulting from the observations made of the children.

The results of administering the MPS at the intervention and comparison early childhood settings are set out in Tables 4.2 and 4.3.

Table 4.2 *Pre- and post-assessment scores for Intervention settings 1 and 2*

Items	1: Space and resources		2: Adults engaging in movement		3: Planning from observations	
Babies	**I1**	**I2**	**I1**	**I2**	**I1**	**I2**
Pre-assessment results	4	4	2	3	4	2
Post-assessment results	4	5	4	4	4	3
Toddlers	**I1**	**I2**	**I1**	**I2**	**I1**	**I2**
Pre-assessment results	4	4	2	2	4	2
Post-assessment results	4	6	4	4	4	4
Preschool	**I1**	**I2**	**I1**	**I2**	**I1**	**I2**
Pre-assessment results	4	3	3	2	3	3
Post-assessment results	4	3	4	4	3	3

Key:
I 1 = Intervention setting 1
I 2 = Intervention setting 2

Scores:
1 = inadequate 3 = minimal 5 = good 7 = excellent

Table 4.3 *Pre- and post-assessment scores for Comparison settings 1 and 2*

Items	1: Space and resources		2: Adults engaging in movement		3 Planning from observations	
Babies	**C1**	**C2**	**C1**	**C2**	**C1**	**C2**
Pre-assessment results	4	4	2	3	4	4
Post-assessment results	4	4	2	3	4	4
Toddlers	**C1**	**C2**	**C1**	**C2**	**C1**	**C2**
Pre-assessment results	3	2	2	2	4	3
Post-assessment results	3	3	2	2	4	3
Preschool	**C1**	**C2**	**C1**	**C2**	**C1**	**C2**
Pre-assessment results	3	3	2	2	3	3
Post-assessment results	3	3	2	2	3	3

Key:
C 1 = Comparison setting 1
C 2 = Comparison setting 2

Scores:
1 = inadequate 3 = minimal 5 = good 7 = excellent

Item 1: Space and resources
The results for Intervention setting 2 (I2)
The baby room and toddler room at Intervention setting 2 (I2)   The findings for Item 1: Space and resources presented in Table 4.2, show that the baby room and toddler room at Intervention setting 2 increased their scores from 4 to 5 (good) and 6 (better than good), respectively, after the intervention. Interestingly, on the day of the training, members of staff working in the toddler room at the setting, keen to rearrange their physical space, set about implementing changes, and reorganising equipment and materials, providing a dedicated space for movement-play with seven pieces of equipment and materials.

Both baby and toddler rooms post training had more resources accessible each day than previously, encouraging the children to move in a variety of ways, indoors and outdoors. Resources for babies included a baby gym, soft mats, a tunnel, soft play shapes, chiffon scarves and pillows (see Figures 4.1, 4.2 and 4.3).

Figure 4.1 *Baby gym accessible to infants at all times*

Figure 4.2 *Soft play equipment with mats, which are useful for all age groups*

After the intervention, the toddlers were engaged in challenging activities, such as spinning, climbing and jumping off equipment indoors. Furthermore, the organisation of the toddler room enabled the children to spontaneously participate in movement activities alone or with their peers or adults.

Figure 4.3 *A clear tunnel with cushions and chiffon scarves set on top of large mats*

All the rooms at the setting had sufficient floor space available – at least 50 per cent – for movement activities.

The preschool room at Intervention setting 2 (I2)   The manager resisted changes to the preschool room post training, but made available an adjacent room that was to be dedicated to movement activities on a regular basis. Consequently, the resources in the room were not easily accessible to the children in the group – they were only available when the adult led the group in the second room. This did take place on a regular basis, however.

Resources consisted of a large cotton-covered elastic, ribbon sticks, a spinning cone, small soft balls, Lycra material, body balls, soft play shapes and mats (see Figure 4.4). The movement activities that took place included spinning, rolling, tug of war, jumping, tummy crawling and dancing.

The results for Intervention setting 1 (I1)

The scores for Intervention setting 1 remained at 4 before and after the intervention, which is just above the minimal score for this item. This was due to the setting having to share the resources with each of the other rooms, limiting children's access to them.

Figure 4.4 *Cotton-covered elastic, small soft balls, ribbon sticks and Lycra material*

The baby room and toddlers room at Intervention setting 1 (I1)   Staff in the baby room made greater use of their existing resources and bought additional resources post training, though some of these were shared with the other rooms. They arranged cushions and soft play resources so that they were easily accessible to the babies, improved the attractiveness of an area with pretty materials and cushions and provided chiffon scarves and a shallow rocker. Staff sometimes utilised the space on the floor to enhance babies' movement experiences.

Initially, staff in the toddler room tended to do whole group movement activities, but gradually over the four weeks they organised their room and resources to enable the children to spontaneously move in a variety of ways, such as spinning, jumping, stretching, rocking, tummy crawling, crawling on all fours and turning upside down.

Sometimes an adult would lead the children into the activity by suggesting that they lie on their backs and roll over on to their tummies or spin around. Other adults were observed rocking a child while singing a lullaby, while others could be seen lifting toddlers upside down.

Children were engaged in challenging and vigorous activities indoors, but not outdoors.

The preschool room at Intervention setting 1 (I1)   Staff changes, as well as absences on the training day resulted in a slow start for the preschool room at this setting. Eventually, however, the members of staff set up large soft play shapes, a climbing frame and mats indoors (see Figures 4.5, 4.6 and 4.7).

Figures 4.5 and 4.6   *Large soft play shapes to climb and jump from onto large mats*

Figure 4.7   *Climbing frame suitable for use indoors*

Vigorous activities took place as the children repeatedly climbed to the top of the large soft cube and jumped onto the mats. These children made independent decisions based on their experiences about how the soft play shapes should be arranged and where the mats should be placed in relation to their anticipation of their landing place. Thus, the organisation of the environment encouraged socialisation between all the children as movement conversations took place as well as verbal communication, such as 'I'm going to jump right over there', or they reorganised the resources, saying, for example, 'Let's move the mats', or they let others know how they felt: 'I don't like the noise'.

The adults allowed the children the space and time to practise, rehearse and revise their movement activities as they engaged with each other about how they could adapt their environment to suit their needs.

Outdoors   Outdoor equipment was stored in a shed or brought out from inside, including a climbing frame, slide, blocks and a spinning cone, bikes and balancing beams. The equipment was not always set up each day, however, and therefore was infrequently available for the children to use.

This lack of accessibility to challenging activities meant that the children had fewer opportunities to engage in physically demanding play outdoors, so the scores for this item remained at 4, which is below good, for all the rooms.

The results for the comparison settings

Even though the toddler room at Comparison setting 2 (C2) slightly increased its score because it acquired some resources, all the other comparison settings' scores remained the same – just above minimal or below – for the duration of the study.

The scores were low partly because of the lack of space available for movement, but also because of the limited availability of materials and equipment, as well as a lack of adult engagement in movement with the children. For example, the resources consisted of only pillows and tumbling mats in one setting. Furthermore, with regard to adult engagement, one practitioner commented that, 'we have lots of children so we don't really do this', referring to movement activities, and another said they did this, 'every Friday afternoon'.

Thus, space and resources were not freely available to the children, which affected their opportunities to move every day. The children at Comparison setting 1 (C1) had limited outdoor equipment and none that enabled them to engage in moderate or challenging activities. They went to a nearby park 'once' or 'twice' a month.

Item 2: Adults engaging in movement with the children

In Tables 4.1 and 4.2, we can see that all the rooms at both the intervention and comparison settings received a minimal or below minimal score for this item prior to the intervention. These results reflect the fact that practitioners adopted a non-interactive, observational approach at all the settings at that stage.

Comments made by the practitioners in response to questions about joining children in their movement-play included, 'adults don't join babies in their movement-play', while other members of staff working with different age groups responded, 'I observe', 'I make sure they are safe' and 'We create the space for movement and the adults stand in specific areas' and observe children in their play outdoors.

The scores for the comparison settings for this item did not change during the course of the study.

The results for Intervention settings 1 (I1) and 2 (I2)

After training, support and advice were given at the intervention settings, their scores increased from minimal and below to 4, which is moving towards good, for all age groups. The post-assessment results further indicate that the majority of adults at the intervention settings were encouraging (3.2), initiating (3.3), prompting and joining (5.1) the children in their movement activities after the training.

These results indicate that most adults were taking on a more interactive role in their engagement with children in movement activities after the intervention. By engaging with children in their movement-play, these adults adopted a Vygotskian (Daniels, 2001) perspective on their role post training. This was not always the case for adults who did not attend the training. Similarly, staff at the comparison settings, which did not receive training, did not join children in their movement activities.

Implementation of the intervention

At Intervention setting 1 (I1), mats and cushions were arranged on the floor of the preschool room, which gave children opportunities to roll around, jump and tumble together.

One member of staff joined the children in their movement-play, taking an interest in what they were doing and, where appropriate, moving with them. Another staff member, who had not attended training, took on a supervisory role, thwarting children's attempts at tumbling play. The children were told to 'stop fighting' when, in fact, they were doing very crucial rough and tumble activities, essential for the healthy development of the 'emotional brain and its connections to the forebrain, which are heavily involved in impulse control and behaviour' (Goddard Blythe, 2005c: 186). This staff member, however, as mentioned, viewed these tumbling activities as fighting rather than more vigorous but safe play, as she had not been introduced to the benefits of these movement activities and therefore had missed out on the discussions that had taken place during the training. Her colleague, who had attended the training, observed, encouraged and moved resources when needed.

A skilful practitioner in the baby room at Intervention setting 2 (I2) was able to cascade what she had learnt during the training to her colleagues, who were receptive and keen to apply this knowledge to their practice. Thus, the babies were provided with opportunities for floor play and other movement-play activities in their two rooms. These included rocking the babies, pulling a baby lying on gold lamé material along the floor, crawling through a tunnel, climbing over and down soft play shapes, climbing and sliding on the baby gym.

In the preschool room at Intervention setting 2, where a separate room for movement was set up after the training session, a practitioner invited small groups of children to join her in directed movement activities, such as spinning, rolling, tug of war, jumping, tummy crawling and dancing, for two half-hour sessions each day. One child was able to spin the spinning cone independently after practising this during an afternoon session.

Children in the preschool and toddler rooms at both the intervention settings were engaged in vigorous activities on their own or with their peers or adults inside, but not outdoors.

Babies did not engage in vigorous activities indoors at Intervention setting 1 or outside at either of the settings. The members of staff were reluctant to safely turn babies upside down or swing them high in the air or provide equipment for safely climbing up, over and down, for example.

Challenging activities for preschool children outdoors were unavailable because of an absence of equipment such as A-frames and ladders, monkey bars, climbing walls, trees for climbing, wheelbarrows for transporting heavy equipment and bricks. Consequently, they had very few opportunities to be active in physically demanding play outdoors.

A disinclination on the part of some staff at both settings to actively put babies on their tummies resulted in those babies who were not yet crawling being propped up with cushions or held by an adult on their lap. Staff were advised to lie on the floor with the babies on their tummies, facing the babies, making eye contact and placing interesting items just out of the babies' reach. This was advised as babies are more likely to develop movement from this position than from a sedentary sitting position if they have not yet become mobile.

Movement activities observed indoors for babies eventually included tummy crawling, with space being made available for them to crawl on all fours, as well as spinning in a shallow cone, jumping, rocking and rolling. Babies sometimes independently explored their space and resources, while at other times adults joined them, giving them attention and support.

The majority of staff at Intervention setting 1 joined the babies in their movement-play post intervention. Before, only the room leader did so.

The range of activities offered to babies outdoors compared to those available indoors was limited in scope at both settings and no activities were vigorous.

At Intervention setting 2, an adult in the toddler room commented that movement-play activities had 'energised' both the staff and the children, saying also that the children 'seek out every activity they can' and are 'bonding a lot more together as friends and play more together as a group'. She also said that her bond with the children was 'stronger' as a result. Another member of staff said that, when she was on the floor moving with the children, she saw things 'from their point of view'.

Adults at Intervention setting 2 sometimes joined the toddlers while they were spinning, crawling, rolling, climbing, sliding, playing tug of war and dancing. The members of staff commented at the first follow-up visit that they had had a 'wonderful' morning, the room was more 'interesting' and the children 'really enjoyed' the movement activities. All the practitioners agreed that the room was more appropriate for this age group post training, and as a consequence they had had a 'purposeful' day. The parents also commented on the room, saying that it 'looked much more fun'.

Item 3: Planning for movement from observations of the children

The results for this item for Intervention setting 1 and both the comparison settings remained the same over the period of the study. Comparison setting 1 (C1), however, scored more consistently for this item, with the majority of the rooms scoring 4, which is above minimal, whereas Intervention setting 2, for example, had scores ranging from 2, which is below minimal, to 3, minimal, prior to the intervention.

Comparison setting 1 already had a robust system of observation and planning that all practitioners were required to keep up to date for each child. This did not, however, guarantee that the adults engaged with children in their activities. Instead, as they were required to fulfil the setting's policy regarding observational requirements, they gave these written observations priority over interactions with the children.

Intervention setting 1 (I1)   Observations were carried out regularly at Intervention setting 1, indoors and outdoors, but these did not necessarily lead to related actions in their written planning. Thus, there was a lack of planning for individual children and portfolios did not include the progress that children were making in movement-play over time. Staff commented that planning was focused on resources being made 'available each day', adding that 'children move anyway, they crawl, run, and dance', suggesting that planning for movement activity wasn't essential as children did these things anyway. Consequently, staff were not tracking children's progress, nor planning for their individual needs.

Intervention setting 2 (I2)

The baby room at Intervention setting 2 increased its score from 2, below minimal, to 3, minimal, as the staff recorded some observations for the children's portfolios that were sometimes used in planning.

   The toddler room at Intervention setting 2 increased its score from 2, below minimal, to 4, towards good, after the intervention because members of staff were recording observations of individual children and planning for their specific needs and interests.

CASE STUDY

During the training day, we discussed a child who frequently sought to escape from the toddler room at Intervention setting 2 and was reluctant to play with her peers. She was observed frequently rocking to and fro, rarely interacting with other children or adults, neither playing nor communicating with them, prior to the intervention. She was either unable to express her thoughts and feelings or was disinclined to, and instead would frequently attempt to open the door and leave the room.

At the training session staff described this child's behaviour, expressing their concerns, and we discussed possible responses to these and her rocking movements. It was agreed that provision would be made for her to participate in vestibular activities, such as spinning, sliding and climbing, to satisfy her movement needs.

After the training session, the room was reorganised and additional equipment and resources were provided. Within the first week after introducing movement-play to the children, this child was observed responding enthusiastically to the movement opportunities available. She began to move and play alongside her peers, interacting and communicating with other children and adults, and ceased to rock to and fro. She also did not attempt to escape from the room again!

After implementing the movement-play activities, staff noticed that the behaviour of all the children changed. The staff in the room at intervention setting 2 had radically changed their environment at the training session, devoting significant space to movement. The organisation of the space and resources enabled these children to move freely, without interrupting other toddlers engaged in more sedentary activities in different areas within the room. Consequently, staff members were able to observe and notice individual development more as they no longer had to deal with the disruption that had occurred previously when space for movement had been limited or it had been placed inappropriately close to areas where quieter activities had been arranged within the room. This helped them with their planning, too.

The preschool room at Intervention setting 2 (I2)
Observations in the preschool room at Intervention setting 2 showed that children were increasing their skills in using the equipment by being given uninterrupted opportunities to practise. Staff commented that the children 'chat to each other a lot more' during movement-play activities. Staff noticed that the children 'really like' the movement sessions, saying that 'they like small group time' and ask if they can go into the movement room. Staff also observed the children participating in more adventurous play outdoors since indoor movement activities had been implemented.

The members of staff seemed to be observing children from a new perspective, post training. During the training session, a practitioner discussed a child she described as 'disorganised', who 'found it hard to stay still' and 'focused' and 'moved constantly'. After the training session, this child's needs were considered from a movement perspective and the practitioner responded by encouraging her to do tummy crawling, crawling, rolling, swinging and spinning in order to satisfy this child's need to be constantly physically active. The staff were not regularly observing and responding to or planning for children's individual movement needs and interests, however. Some observations were verbally expressed, while others were recorded in children's portfolios and sometimes used in planning.

The post-assessment results for this item may be attributed to the following three factors.

1) Indicator 5.1 for Item 3 of the MPS (see the table near the beginning of this chapter) requires practitioners to regularly observe children's specific responses to movement activities and write plans suited to their needs and interests (indicator 5.2). This level of good practice requires a deep knowledge and understanding of movement-play, which takes time to

develop. During this short study, staff focused their energies on implementing newly acquired knowledge in their setting, learning new ways to work with the children, and sometimes noticed children's responses. The duration of the study allowed little time for further reading and training. Moreover, the four-week follow-up period did not allow sufficient time to advise and support staff fully in the arts of observation and planning.

2) After the training, members of staff occasionally shared observations with parents about their children's physical activity, what kinds of things they did at home and the setting (see indicator 5.3, Item 3 of the MPS). This started to happen on a more regular basis after a meeting with staff and parents took place, once the study had finished, about the importance of movement-play.

3) Indicator 5.4, Item 3 of the MPS, requires that 'Children's portfolios include their progress in movement-play with photos and/or written observations'. Movement-play was new to the staff involved in this study and the duration of the study was too short for staff to gain sufficient knowledge and experience in order to action this point consistently for all the children.

The graph in Figure 4.8 shows the mean pre- and post-assessment scores for each age group at the intervention and comparison settings.

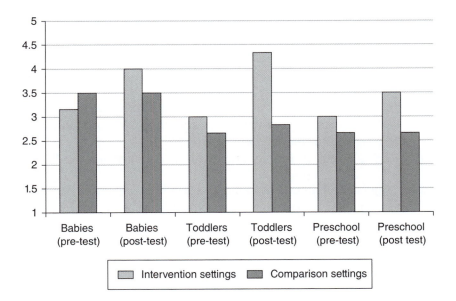

Figure 4.8 *Results for intervention and comparison settings (mean scores of items)*

In summary, the quantitative results illustrated in Figure 4.8 show that the intervention settings increased their scores well for all three items, while the scores for the comparison settings remained the same, with the exception of a slight increase for the toddler room at C2 only, accounted for by the acquisition of some additional resources.

Qualitative data

Qualitative data gathered via unstructured interviews revealed that the manager at Intervention setting 1 found the rooms 'calmer' after the training session, with staff 'enjoying their work a lot more' as they 'engaged in movement-play with the children'. The children's 'behaviour' was 'better because staff were moving and playing with the children more' and the children were therefore 'responding to staff a lot more'.

The manager said that there were 'benefits' for the two children with special needs, as they were now more physically active, as well as for all the staff and children. Most adults at both the intervention settings were taking an active role with the children in their movement-play and some made astute observations. The manager at Intervention setting 2 thought that their success in implementing movement-play was largely due to all the staff receiving training at the same time, which she considered more effective than sending one or two members of staff for external training.

As the staff began implementing movement-play in their settings, interviews revealed a degree of understanding about the links between movement and specific areas of development. For example, members of staff said that movement-play is important for children's 'motor development', 'coordination', 'balance', 'behaviour' and 'concentration'.

The findings of this small study illustrate that training and follow-up support and advice can make a difference to:

- practitioner knowledge and understanding of movement-play
- the role of adults, with practitioners adopting a Vygotskian interactive role based on the children's interests
- children's sharing of movement conversations with peers and adults.

As a consequence, children's movement experiences improved, which, it is anticipated, will have a positive impact on their learning and development.

Discussion

The variations in the findings indicate that the MPS has some validity. The overall findings showed that an intervention did improve the quality of the environment and practice.

The results indicated that the intervention had consistent outcomes in terms of the adults engaging in movement with the children across the study. Practitioners were willing to take a more active role with the children post intervention, being prepared to move freely with children, sometimes engaging in shared movement conversations. This improvement in the quality of the role of the adults led to the children expanding their movement repertoire. This suggests that, after the intervention, most adults at Intervention settings 1 and 2 adopted a Vygotskian interactive role, engaging with the children and becoming active agents with them, developing their movement experiences.

Contrastingly, adults at Comparison settings 1 and 2 tended to take on more of an observational role, and consequently their scores remained at below minimal over the same period of time.

These findings indicate that the intervention did make a significant difference to children's movement experiences, which resulted from the improvement in the quality of the adults' engagement in movement with the children.

Conclusion

After the intervention, it was apparent that the children were given the 'space, time and the conditions' advocated by Goddard Blythe (2005c: 175), as well as the encouragement they needed to engage in movement activities.

The first five years in children's lives are critical for their social interactions and language and cognitive development. Such developmental outcomes, it has been found, are significantly related to the quality of preschool settings (Sylva et al., 2006). Influenced by the EPPE study, we developed the MPS specifically to assess quality in settings catering for children from birth to the age of six.

This study found that a targeted intervention consisting of training, support and advice resulted in enhanced movement experiences for young children. Our findings shed light on the importance of the quality of the environment and pedagogy. In this respect, the study is valuable as it highlights the effects of an appropriate, targeted intervention on children's movement activities, as well as measures of quality related to an intervention.

There appears to be a paucity of research on measuring quality in this area. This study therefore attempted to make a contribution to addressing this by developing and using the MPS.

Further reading

Harms, T., Clifford, R. and Cryer, D. (2005) *Early Childhood Environment Rating Scale Revised Edition* (ECERS-R). New York: Teacher's College Press.

Harms, T., Cryer, D. and Clifford, R. (2006) *Infant/Toddler Environment Rating Scale, Revised Edition* (ITERS-R). New York: Teacher's College Press.

MacNaughton, G., Rolfe, S.A., Siraj-Blatchford, I. (2010) *Doing Early Childhood Research: International perspectives on theory and practice* (Second Edition). Maidenhead: Open University Press.

Sylva, K., Melhuish, E., Sammons, P., Siraj-Blatchford, I. and Taggart, B. (2012) 'Effective Pre-School, Primary and Secondary Education Project (EPPSE 3–14): influences on students' development from age 11–14'. Research Brief DFE-RB202. London: Department for Education.

Sylva, K., Melhuish, E., Sammons. P., Siraj-Blatchford, I., Taggart, B. and Elliot, K. (2004) 'The Effective Provision of Pre-school Education (EPPE) Project: Findings from pre-school to end of Key Stage 1'. Institute of Education, University of London, University of Oxford, Birkbeck, University of London and Sure Start for the Department for Education and Skills. Nottinghan: DfES Publications.

Sylva, K., Siraj-Blatchford, I. and Taggart, B. (2006) *Assessing Quality in the Early Years: Early Childhood Environment Rating Scale Extension (ECERS-E): Four curricular subscales*. Stoke-on-Trent: Trentham Books.

Sylva, K., Siraj-Blatchford, I. and Taggart, R. (2010) *ECERS-E: The Early Childhood Environment Rating Scale Curricular Extension to ECERS-R*. Stoke-on-Trent: Trentham Books.

5
Working with families to promote movement-play

Introduction

The early years of children's lives are the foundation that shape their future health, growth, development and learning. Many factors influence children's development, including, social, cultural, genetic and prenatal factors, illness, poverty, nutrition and life events. The structure and development of young children's brains, as we have seen in Chapter 1, are shaped by the co-action of both genes and environmental influences and their interaction with that environment (Rutter, 2006a).

In Chapter 4 we referred to the relationship between the quality of the early childhood educational environment and children's learning and development, highlighting the impact of high-quality provision on children's socio-behavioural development, cognitive progress and academic skills. The effect of high-quality care and education on children's outcomes is therefore significant, but it is the home learning environment (HLE) that has been found to have one of the greatest impacts on young children's development (Melhuish et al., 2001; 2008).

This is important information for the early childhood setting as it strongly suggests that parents and carers are key people in their children's early experiences. One of the most effective approaches to improving children's lives, therefore, is to support parents in actively engaging with children's learning at home, especially in the early years (Desforges and Abouchaar, 2003; Siraj-Blatchford and Siraj-Blatchford, 2009; Sylva et al., 2004).

Chapter 6 addresses the importance of ensuring that parents are included in the process of developing a physical development (inclusive of movement-play) policy.

The family in the UK today

The family structure in the UK has been undergoing constant change over the last few decades and today consists of myriad different units. In 2012, the Office for National Statistics revealed that families with dependent children consisted of married couples, cohabiting couples and single parents. It is no longer unusual for children to be involved in complicated family structures and this includes stepfamilies, parents living apart and sharing their children's care, parents of the same gender and extended families. In addition, there are increasing numbers of looked after children, adoptive parents and foster carers.

A study conducted for the Department for Education by Siraj-Blatchford et al. (2011: 67) shows the influence of wider family members, such as an older sibling, aunt, uncle and grandparents, in children's lives today. Thus, a wide range of family members other than mothers, fathers or primary carers are increasingly involved in children's early care and education. For the purposes of this chapter, 'parents' are defined as all those involved in the care of young children.

Today's society is increasingly diverse, economically, socially and culturally, which impacts on the family unit and the ways in which life can be lived (Knowles, 2009). Families may be indigenous to the UK, they may be wealthy professionals, educated middle-class, working-class, unemployed and referred to as advantaged or disadvantaged, depending on levels of income. Increasing numbers of families today are living in relative poverty. Families may be from a variety of ethnic backgrounds, including second- or third-generation immigrants who feel a sense of belonging to an ethnic community as well as the UK. Some families may have recently migrated to the UK, either voluntarily or under extenuating circumstances, with the consequence of their having little social support.

Many early childhood settings' intakes include children from a wide range of countries and cultures. They may have many varied experiences and their families may hold a variety of beliefs and values, practise different religions and speak a number of languages. Staff at early childhood settings will, therefore, also need to be aware of the diversity of practices among their parents and carers and that the 'universal goals of parenting can be accomplished in many different ways' (Pachter and Dumont-Matheiu, 2004: 88).

Risk and resilience

Within these diverse family structures, the children's experiences will be quite varied as they and their parents and carers make adjustments and adapt to their circumstances, influenced by their individual characteristics and the society in which they live (Pachter and Dumont-Mathieu, 2004).

The parental role is wideranging, encompassing the most fundamental aim, which is to ensure the survival and development of their children. Most parents strive to do their best within the circumstances in which they find themselves and want the best for their children. Some parents are better off and may give their children an advantage that others are not able to, while other parents may find themselves in less advantageous circumstances due to a variety of social, economic or personal reasons. Such adversities may affect parental behaviours and be reflected in what they do with their children. Families may therefore encounter a number of factors that can disrupt their children's early development, from the time of conception to birth and beyond. These may include financial insecurity, poor housing, malnutrition and deficiencies in health.

Poor early experiences related to physical and psychological care, illness, a lack of bonding and attachment, poor relationships with siblings and others, inadequate stimulation and social deprivation, are all considered to be risk factors and predictors of children's learning outcomes in the early years (Siraj-Blatchford and Siraj-Blatchford, 2009: 17). Some of these risk factors are thought to be more difficult to overcome than others and can therefore present families with many overwhelming challenges.

Despite experiencing risks, some families, nevertheless, are able to overcome the accompanying stress and adversity and achieve a good outcome (Rutter, 2006b). The focus more recently has been on this resilience that some individuals and families show in the face of adversity (Edwards and Apostolov, 2007; Rutter, 2006b). Some just find a way to successfully cope with the challenge, stress or hardship they are faced with and resilience plays a part in that outcome.

It is likely that most parents will want to reduce the risks their children face, manage their lives and promote resilience. Some children have been found to be capable of coping with serious adversity, while others have struggled with minor risks (Kaplan and Owens, 2004). Nonetheless, exposure to risk is not always a bad thing as such experiences may help individuals to develop coping mechanisms. There is evidence that stressful or adverse experiences can, in some instances, actually strengthen resistance to later stress (Rutter, 2006b).

Counteracting risks to children and the home learning environment (HLE)

Siraj-Blatchford and Siraj-Blatchford (2009: 13) identified two areas of resilience (protective factors) to counter risks to children that can influence their outcomes:

1. Parental interest and involvement in education, having expectations and promoting self-efficacy (a belief that one's desires are achievable).
2. Providing additional educational support through an enhanced early home learning environment.

The EPPE (Sylva et al., 2004) research confirmed the importance of the child's early years experiences and found that the combination of home, preschool and primary school to be a powerful influence in improving children's learning. Examination of the HLE revealed that children with a positive early HLE achieve more in their early years and throughout primary school (Coghlan et al., 2009) than those who don't. Furthermore, the influence of a high-quality HLE for young children was found to be related to positive behaviour, independence and sociability.

What does a positive high-quality HLE look like?

Siraj-Blatchford (2004) defines a positive HLE as one in which the parents or carers take part in learning activities with their children. The activities parents engaged in at home in the EPPE research included reading to children, playing with letters and numbers, taking children to the library, painting, drawing, teaching children nursery rhymes and songs, taking children on visits and arranging for children to play with their friends. Such activities were found to provide children with an HLE that strongly impacted on outcomes. The EPPE research quite clearly shows that it is what parents and carers *do* with their children that makes a difference to children's outcomes (Sylva et al., 2004).

Furthermore, parents and carers who encourage positive relationships with their children affect their outcomes. As they interact with the children and help them solve problems, they can have a positive effect on them by encouraging metacognition and self-regulation (Siraj-Blatchford and Siraj-Blatchford, 2009). Parents and carers can help their children to become responsible for the consequences of their behaviour by setting appropriate developmental limits, and encouraging independence, empathy and compassion, which will affect the children's social and behavioural outcomes.

The role of the early childhood setting

It is through the provision of early childhood settings promoting a supportive HLE that we can begin to address the gap between advantaged and disadvantaged children and counter the effects of the risks described above in the early years and beyond.

Supporting families with children who are at risk of later underachievement can be undertaken through raising the quality of the HLE, as well as addressing issues of bonding and attachment and improving social relationships and behaviour. If this is the case then, pre-school and school settings that do not promote parental support and positive HLEs are missing an important element in raising achievement (Sylva et al., 2008).

Research and policy are sending the same message

Government policies have been introduced in response to this knowledge in order to drive improvement in parental involvement in their children's early education. In 2004, the government acknowledged the strength of the parental role through its Every Child Matters agenda and, later, in 2007, Every Parent Matters, as parents are considered the child's first and most enduring educators.

In 2011, the Department for Education and Department of Health produced a document on behalf of the coalition government entitled, 'Supporting families in the Foundation years', which advocates that providers strengthen their engagement with parents. Ofsted's first ever annual report for the early years sector (2012/13: 5) also emphasises parental involvement as a key factor in helping children learn, with the quality of the HLE being a major factor in 'explaining the differences between children from low-income backgrounds and their wealthier peers'.

Supporting parents to help children learn at home has been consistently promoted in policy and continues to be through the Statutory Framework for the EYFS (DfE, 2014), which highlights the early years sector's role in 'breaking the cycle of disadvantage' (Ofsted, 2012/13: 5).

Working with parents and carers

There is no doubt that working with families in early childhood settings requires skill, much knowledge and confidence on the part of practitioners. Central to working with parents and carers are the ways in which practitioners encourage the children's and families' participation.

An effective setting will ensure that the members of staff develop a consistent relationship with each caregiver, encourage parental involvement, focus on each child as an individual and are knowledgeable about each individual child's development. Furthermore, the early childhood setting will ensure that parents and carers are included in the formation of their physical development policy, as outlined in Chapter 6.

To understand how to develop effective parent and carer partnerships, it is imperative that providers consider how they will reach out to all of them. Some parents and carers are more skilled than others at developing relationships with staff in early education provisions. Other families may need support in approaching the setting, building a relationship and sustaining participation. Once a good relationship has developed between the setting and the family, however, then practitioners are one step further towards influencing the HLE in a positive way (Siraj-Blatchford and Siraj-Blatchford, 2009).

Visits to children in their homes give practitioners an opportunity to see the families on their own 'turf' and build relationships from this valuable starting point. Home visits enable the setting to identify each family's strengths and work together with the parents or carers and the children to reshape any path of risk that may have been identified. This is important if all children are to be supported in their learning and development and ready to make the most of the education system by the time they reach statutory school age (Siraj-Blatchford and Siraj-Blatchford, 2009).

Movement-play and home visits

An important starting point for developing strong partnerships with parents can be undertaking home visits. Home visits should be non-judgemental and well planned and may begin with family support services, the baby feeding team or health visitors supporting families. These services may also talk to parents about the importance of movement and its influence on their children's health and development. Some parents may not be aware of the significance of tummy time for a baby's development or that the floor is the best playground for a young infant or how this movement pattern will support development to crawling and, even, learning in school later on.

Visits to the home environment prior to enrolment at the early education setting will provide an opening for practitioners to observe and discuss with the parents or carers the children's experiences of being physically active. Observations of each infant in his or her home may reveal their expertise in early movement patterns or their reluctance to move without adult help. Preschool-age children may talk about physical activities that they enjoy, can do alone, resist or prefer an adult to support them with. Such discussions with parents or carers may help build a more rounded picture of the infants' or young children's early movement patterns, their experiences, attitudes and the challenges they seek indoors and outdoors.

Customs and practices

The best way to find out about parenting practices is to ask parents and carers directly and note the diversity and similarity for the parents and carers of the children at the setting.

Parents and carers will adopt different customs and practices, giving their infants' different early experiences. For example, in their first few months, babies may be transported in a pram or a carry seat from the car to the home or early years setting or carried in a sling on the back or front of the parent or carer. Such practices for transporting infants may be the result of a long-standing cultural custom or a recent change. For example, it is common practice for parents in many countries such as South America, Africa, Asia and elsewhere, to carry an infant in material strapped on to their mother's and sometimes their father's front or back. Migrant parents often continue customs from home in their host country. Some indigenous parents in the UK have also adopted this custom and will carry their baby in slings rather than use a pram or pushchair. The motion that babies experience when being carried around by an adult enhances their vestibular system and provides an enriched environment of warmth and comfort in which they can feel safe and secure, enhancing the attachment between parent or carer and child.

Many Eastern cultures have routinely practised baby massage as a normal part of a new baby's life, such as in many parts of India. More recently, this has become increasingly popular with parents in the UK, as well as staff at early childhood education settings. Parents or carers and babies spend quality time together, interacting through the nurturing touch of massage, which calms babies' nervous systems, bringing the benefits of bonding and communication, too (Sunderland, 2007). Through massage, babies and parents or carers connect and form an attachment with each other in a safe and secure atmosphere. A secure attachment with a carer can protect children against adverse outcomes and help them to develop social competence and peer relations (Soliday, 2004).

A few decades ago, it was customary for new babies in the UK to be pushed in a coach-style pram, with sophisticated suspension and padded mattresses, giving babies not only a comfortable ride but also stimulation of their vestibular system. There are many benefits to babies lying flat in a pram, not least the healthy development of their spines.

Though built to last, these transport systems have been replaced by more convenient collapsible pram-pushchairs, which can consist of a small pram unit, a seat unit and/or a car seat. Some of these, however, tend to restrict infants' ability to stretch out, lie on their backs or roll from side to side, which they were able to do in the more bulky coach-style prams or pram units because these allowed babies to lie flat, giving them the freedom to move, kick their legs and wave their arms around, searching for early movement patterns. All these movements are essential for infants' early development, but they cannot do them while confined in restrictive containers.

Obviously, car seats are vital for the safety of infants when they are travelling in cars, but, while car seats and other carrying devices enable babies to be moved easily, they do not allow babies to move easily while they are in them (Lamont, 2007b). The length of time a baby's spontaneous movements are contained should be minimised to enable optimum physical development to take place.

Newborn babies need the loving arms of their parents and carers; they need to feel the heartbeat, reassuring touch and warmth of their mothers. When not in the loving arms of another human being or asleep, babies need to be lying flat on their tummies or backs rather than confined in any equipment that restricts their ability to flex their limbs and move their heads. While lying on a soft rug or sheepskin, an infant can, from this position, seek out movements that they are naturally programmed to do as they develop and grow (Lamont, 2007b).

As their bodies grow stronger, babies will try to lift one hip and then the other, beginning their movement journey from stationary to rolling over from their backs to their fronts and vice versa. In time, babies move on their tummies, going round and round or even backwards and, eventually, reach out for their favourite toys maybe, then move forwards.

All these little developmental steps can be hard work for infants and take time to perfect. Parents and carers need to be on their tummies, too, joining their infants, making eye contact, talking to them and seeing the world from their viewpoint. A suitable surface, such as a wooden floor, enables babies to move around easily to do all that they need to do. Babies deserve lots of praise and applause for moving independently for the first time and reaching this milestone in their development.

Parents and carers joining in with their infants' movement-play provide vital opportunities for sociable, interactive times together. The first months of infants' lives are when they are often keenly interested in the faces of their parents or carers as they are held in loving arms or lay on the floor on tummies together or are rolled gently on a bed, communicating together through touch, movement, laughter, facial expressions, sounds and words. Face-to-face conversations between parents and infants through loving interactions show that the parents are in tune with their babies as they respond to each other's facial gestures, showing sensitivity towards infants in the coming and going of these conversations. This is the beginning of infants experiencing an invaluable route to developing social relationships with others. When a mother holds her baby in her arms, for example, she provides her physical presence for the baby, which allows him or her to hold on to or touch her skin when needing reassurance so that he or she feels secure, which is the foundation to much learning (Lamont, 2009).

Later, babies learn to sit up independently without the need to be propped up or sat in equipment. Sitting a baby in a chair or using any other equipment before they are ready may damage their spines. If babies are not able to sit up by themselves, then they should not be propped up; if they can sit up unsupported, then they do not need equipment to hold them up.

Eventually, after much hard work, babies will be ready to be up on all fours, crawling on hands and knees, exploring their environment. At this time, infants need ample space to move around in, both indoors and outdoors – the floor should be their rehearsal space. These babies have reached another milestone in their movement development that demands more applause for their achievement after such hard work over many months.

The early movement patterns described above are crucial if infants are to gain all the benefits needed for their future development and learning. Infants need time, space and family members to join them on the floor until they are ready to pull themselves up to standing and, eventually, to join the adults in walking, running and playing games.

Modern children's physical activity is constrained in many ways and in a variety of contexts. For example, there has been a considerable decline in outdoor play over the last two decades. Fears related to traffic, 'stranger danger' and less tolerance of young people are all contributing to driving children indoors. An ICM Poll conducted on behalf of Play England (2011) revealed that one in four eight- to ten-year-olds have never played outside without an adult and one in three parents will not allow older children, aged eight to fifteen, to play outside the house or garden. Children today therefore spend less time outside than their parents did as children, yet 80 per cent of children would prefer to play outside and 86 per cent of parents would rather their children go to the park on a nice day than stay indoors watching TV (Play England, 2011).

One of the consequences of this is that children are adopting more sedentary lifestyles and, as a result, significant numbers are becoming overweight or obese and there has been a re-emergence of rickets. The decline in outdoor spaces for children to play has also contributed to them having less freedom to play spontaneously outside than at any other time in our history. Yet, one of the best things for children's health is for them to go outdoors to play (Mackett, 2004) since it is essential to their health, well-being and future life chances (Play England, 2011).

Family members and carers joining young children in physical activities, such as rough and tumble, going to the local park, digging mud in the garden, going on a bike ride, building sandcastles or swimming in the sea, can provide stimulation for the children's imagination as well as challenges that support their physical development. As young children play outside, they develop their physical fitness and strength. By engaging in these physical activities with their children, parents have opportunities to help their children with problemsolving experiences that are encountered and can support them as behavioural problems arise and help resolve conflicts.

Engaging in and enjoying activities such as these not only contributes positively to the children's health and well-being but also provides opportunities for sustained shared interactions between parents or carers and children, strengthening the bond between them.

Getting parents and carers involved

A settings' physical development policy will inform parents and carers about the importance that is placed on all infants and young children being physically active. See Chapter 6 for ways in which parents and carers can be included in developing such a policy and facilitating effective partnerships with them.

During an introductory tour of the setting, prospective parents and carers will also be able to observe the many ways in which the children are moving and being physically active indoors and outdoors. The staff can express to them their expectations that all children will engage in movement activities, pointing out the benefits to children's well-being, health, development and learning. They can draw parents' and carers' attention to the setting's physical development policy and link this area of learning to other curriculum areas.

In this way, when parents and carers then first bring their infant or young child to spend time at the setting, they will already be aware of the emphasis that is placed on the children's physical development through movement-play and the reasons for this. Information about each infant's or young child's early movement patterns could be included on the transition or background information form that parents and carers complete for their child on entry.

Talking to parents and carers about their children's physical experiences at home, listening with interest and engaging in a two-way conversation will value them as equal partners in the children's development. In this way, too, both the members of staff at the setting and parents or carers gain a deeper insight into and understanding of the children.

An example of how one setting gathers information from parents and carers

Below is an example of how one setting gathers information from parents and carers about their children's experiences of physical and movement activity at home. This form is given to each parent or carer to complete and followed up with meetings and displays. The three examples of responses from parents show the kind of information they have shared with the setting. These parents also supplied photos of an activity that two of their children enjoyed at home outdoors.

Physical development

Physical development is, as the wording suggests, about how babies and young children gain control of their bodies, but it also includes how children learn about keeping themselves active and healthy and how they learn to use equipment and materials successfully and safely.

Child's name:

Dear parents, carers,

Please provide us with written information and photos about your child's physical development outside of the Nursery. Let us know her/his favourite activities and what you do to support her/his learning in this area. This information will expand Nursery planning and help us to know you better.

Parents' responses

1. Child A

A has a scooter and a strider bike, which we use a lot.

He loves reading books, using building blocks, Lego and train tracks.

(Continued)

(Continued)

He loves playing with water and splashing in the paddling pool.

I want him to learn colours (he still says everything is red) and shapes and am trying to do this with puzzles and books.

2. Child B

B loves being outdoors regardless of the weather. He has just got his first bike and tries hard to move forwards using his own force, but has not quite got there yet. He also likes his scooter, but struggles a bit to keep his balance. Another favourite pastime is playing in the sand box, filling his bucket using his spade.

During weekends we take him to the children's theatre, which he also enjoys, especially if he gets a chance to participate and play musical instruments.

3. Child C

C loves all sorts of activities. Outside of home, she loves to go to the park: swinging, sliding, climbing and bouncing. She also goes to lots of different soft play centres.

She has swimming lessons once a week and is learning to kick, hold on to the side and go underwater.

She often practises her walking outside and enjoys playing with the balls.

At home, she has a horse that she plays on. She has learnt how to safely go down the stairs and climb down from the bed or couch.

She loves to splash and kick in the bath.

She is learning how to brush her teeth and how to use her hands to sign.

Keeping parents involved

Creating good relationships with parents and carers is vital if children are to settle well and parents and carers feel confident about them engaging in the activities offered at the setting. Holding various meetings, training in or demonstrations of physical activities at the setting keeps families up to date with this area of learning and what pedagogical practice is used at the setting. Meetings need to be held at various times throughout a day or evening to accommodate parents' and carers' working hours. Some parents may be less likely to engage in stimulating activities with their children at home, but they are not necessarily less able to do so. Inviting family members and carers to observe staff modelling effective practice and/or joining children in movement activities enhances everyone's knowledge and understanding of pedagogical approaches that parents and carers can adopt at home. Using a variety of means to involve parents and carers, such as practical activities, video, photos and visual aids of children and adults engaged in movement activities, helps all family members to feel included, particularly those whose first language is not English. Promoting parental involvement and interest in education also helps children overcome risks of underachievement (Siraj-Blatchford and Siraj-Blatchford, 2009: 8).

An increasing number of grandparents and fathers are becoming the primary carers for all or part of the day, so developing effective partnerships involves offering them practical measures to encourage their involvement in early childcare and education, including developing targeted provision that appeals to their interests (Siraj-Blatchford and Siraj-Blatchford, 2009).

Fathers and/or grandfathers need to be addressed explicitly when they collect or drop off their children and activities directed specifically at their interests. Many dads thrive on being physically active with their young children, often feeling very comfortable with this type of play. Physical activity through movement-play offers settings a unique opportunity to focus on fathers – holding special 'fathers' days', for example, when they can use resources to try out various movement patterns in order to understand how children reach each stage of development and progress to the next.

When parents and carers understand why children do the things they do, they often develop better relationships with them.

CASE STUDY

A children's centre held several meetings, initially just for fathers, to talk about movement-play and have a discussion with them about what they did themselves as children.

A film produced by the London Borough of Camden called *Moving, Learning and Growing: The role of movement in child play and development* was also shown, prompting discussions with the

(Continued)

(Continued)

fathers about physical activity. One father commented that, when he was young, he would play quite risky games and remembered playing on scaffolding, climbing quite high and hanging from it, too. He stated categorically, however, that he did not want his son to take the risks he did, although he was relieved to know what he was doing with his son was so helpful and enjoyable, too. He generally took his son on walks and often visited a park where his son could be as energetic as he needed to be, but more safely than was the case in his own young experiences.

This children's centre also invites fathers to join in with the movement activities their children usually undertake at the setting. A leaflet for parents about movement-play produced by the local authority is also given to families.

Incentives to encourage families to be involved may include such things as providing a recording of the child and parent moving together at a session held at the setting or loaning a bag of resources for use at home, which might include ribbon sticks for dancing, Lycra material to stretch and roll inside, soft small balls for rolling on tummies, and chiffon scarves for peek-a-boo. Loaning resources in this way, to use for movement activities at home, for children to use with parents, siblings or grandparents, may be a means of improving the HLE for some families and also improve interactions between family members and the children. As parents join their children in these activities or watch them move and dance with attention and joy, the children feel a sense of self-worth and achievement as their engagement in movement is valued. When grandparents join their grandchildren in activities, there are benefits for the children that are associated with higher levels of cooperation and less anti-social behaviour (Siraj-Blatchford and Siraj-Blatchford, 2009).

Photos and/or drawings of and verbal feedback on how the resources were used and enjoyed can be fed into the children's portfolios or used in displays of photos and text about their movement experiences. Engaging in two-way conversations about children's movement experiences and sharing educational aims with parents encourages them to make 'pedagogical' efforts at home to support their children: 'In settings that encourage continuity of learning between pre-/early primary school and home children have better cognitive outcomes' (Siraj-Blatchford and Siraj-Blatchford, 2009: 41).

Effective settings value parents and carers as equal partners and encourage them to become involved in physical activity at the setting, joining infants and children in activities set up by the members of staff or inviting parents to use any specific skills they have, such as playing an instrument while children move or leading children in dance or yoga or introducing children to new games and songs. Parents and carers may be asked to help with organising 'a physical activity event for families' when activities and resources can be available for parents and carers to try out and/or for staff to demonstrate together with the children.

Much knowledge and skill is required by practitioners to work with families today and influence the quality of children's early HLE. The complexity of modern family life and diversity of family backgrounds mean that members of staff need good professional development to work effectively with parents and carers if they are to close the gap between the advantaged and disadvantaged.

Linking health and education

In some local authorities, a Healthy Lifestyles project has been set up to work alongside education in the drive to improve the health of children and their families. One such project, called 'Little Steps to Healthy Lives' (2013), in one inner London borough runs a programme with early education settings that includes direct delivery of, as well as signposting families to, services including breastfeeding, immunisations, healthy eating, dental health, physical activity through movement-play, and smoking cessation. By adopting an evidence-based approach, this integrated programme aims to reduce health inequalities and improve health outcomes among families in the borough through early intervention.

Part of the project includes training all staff in all children's centres in physical development through movement-play. These centres have successfully followed up this training by engaging with families through a variety of methods, including showing and/or loaning the DVD called *Moving, Learning and Growing* mentioned in the case study earlier, distributing a leaflet specifically designed for parents and carers, running workshops and meetings, drop-ins and crèches, as well as having regular informal discussions with parents and carers about their children's movement interests and development at home and in the setting. This project will be rolled out in the near future to settings in the voluntary and private sectors.

Parent partnership programmes

Successful parental programmes identified by the Parents, Early Years Learning (PEAL) project (2006) were found to be of a high quality, run by confident, well-trained staff who had the ability to build good-quality relationships between themselves, parents and the children. In turn, qualities that parents and carers looked for in terms of support from practitioners (PEAL, 2006) included recognising that all parents have a 'load to carry'; being there for them – good or bad; giving them a chance to explain things; listening very carefully; trust in relationships; never saying, 'you're not doing it right'; not comparing their children unfavourably with others; patience; a reminder of strengths and signposting.

An equal relationship between parents and carers and practitioners depends on building a genuine partnership based on respecting and valuing each other's contributions and grounded in the principles of equality and diversity (PEAL, 2006). Of course, the children themselves are vital to this partnership. Children, parents, carers and practitioners all working together, contributing equally, can strengthen the partnership, thus giving children the best possible experiences in their early years.

PEAL (2006: 5) developed a model for working with parents and carers living in disadvantaged areas in order to support the development of parental involvement in children's early learning. PEAL supports practitioners to reflect on their partnerships with parents and carers and acknowledge what is already taking place at the setting.

The PEAL programme delivers a one-day training course to all staff. The key elements of authentic relationships, communication and partnership are examined and related to current research, looking at what works best and why. PEAL projects aiming to improve the quality of work with families include the 'Making it REAL (Raising Early Achievement in Literacy) early literacy programme', and 'Making Maths Real', which aims to support children's development in literacy and maths.

Feedback from parents about the REAL 2011 programme was very positive, identifying many different ways in which what they learned helped their children afterwards, such as talking to each other more, reading more books with their children, playing more games and writing, and how these had beneficial effects on the children's confidence, concentration and behaviour. Positive feedback also revealed that 'parents and practitioners both cite home visiting as the most important factor in establishing good relationships and commitment' (PEAL, 2009–12: 1). Something similar for movement-play could be devised, modelling it on such programmes.

Other parent partnership interventions/programmes include Peers Early Education Partnership (PEEP), the Family Development Project and Supporting Parents On Kids Education (SPOKES).

The PEEP programme promoted self-esteem and dispositions to learn as well as literacy. This programme was found to have a significant impact on the quality of parents' interactions with their children at one and two years of age (Evangelou et al., 2009). At the age of five, children involved in the programme showed that they had gained a significant advantage in terms of peer acceptance, cognitive competence, physical and general competence and overall self-esteem.

The Family Development Project involved weekly home visits by trained professionals, the outcome of which was increased support for mothers from partners and families, increased maternal responsiveness and secure attachment for children aged two (Heinicke et al., 2001).

The SPOKES intervention enhanced children's reading achievement through parents enjoying reading and singing songs with their children and focusing on children's early reading skills. Parents worked in groups, receiving feedback from others, recording themselves reading with their children and sharing and discussing these recordings with the group.

The team delivering the training to these parents was very experienced in parenting and/or literacy programmes, was supervised and reflected on its running of the groups through video clips assessing how this could improve with support from its skilled tutors, all of which contributed to the success of the intervention.

In an effective partnership, the children, parents or carers and practitioners have an equal relationship. Parents' and carers' involvement in the settings' drive to increase children's physical activity and movement-play is vital – their support and encouragement are central to the children's positive participation in being physically active. As noted, parents and carers can be encouraged to contribute to a setting's physical development policy and, in this way, feel valued as equal partners.

The content of this chapter will also support settings when developing a physical development policy, as discussed in Chapter 6.

Further activities parents can do at home with their children

What parents and carers do at home with their child/ren plays a vital role in their development, keeps them healthy and happy, and helps develop social skills and build stronger bones and a healthy heart.

The best experiences that parents can give their children to contribute positively to their health and well-being are the simplest everyday things, such as walking together to the shops or to and from the early years setting rather than going by car or taking their children in pushchairs. Children who are encouraged to walk tend to be more active outdoors. Outdoor activities such as playing, walking, cycling and swimming can significantly contribute to the amount of physical activity children do, which can lead to healthier lives (Mackett, 2013).

Interestingly, research by Mackett and Paskins (2008: 8) shows that 'playing provides more physical activity than organised clubs', illustrating that unstructured outdoor play is more beneficial for children's health than organised sports. Parents would do well to walk with their children to the local park or take them further afield where they can enjoy the freedom of running and playing ball games with their friends and use the apparatus in the park to swing, slide and climb. It's free and healthy and anyone can do this. The more physically active parents and carers are, the more their children tend to be also.

Figure 5.1 *Mum and daughter coming down slide at a favourite park of theirs*

The overall message, therefore, is that everyday activities, such as unstructured free play outdoors and walking, significantly increase children's physical activity levels, with benefits for their health. Conversely, the cost to children's well-being and health of *decreasing* physical activity levels is high, yet some of the solutions are quite simple and cheap.

Right from the start, parents and carers can encourage their infants to be physically active indoors by joining them on the floor to play or, when babies are ready to move, provide tunnels for them to crawl through or empty boxes to hide inside or cushions to roll over.

Bathtimes can be fun, too, with parents or carers gently splashing and singing. Also, they can attend dedicated swimming sessions at the local pool for parents and carers and babies.

Toddlers love to be active when singing action rhymes and songs or dancing with their mums or dads or playing with bubbles, streamers, balloons and inviting friends home to play. Some young children, boys and girls, enjoy rough and tumbling or playing with small world toys, building dens using sheets and chairs, playing hide and seek, dressing up and messy play, such as painting or collage, and drawing with chalks on large pieces of paper (lining paper is useful for these activities) or pavements and so on outside.

It is important that parents and carers help their babies and young children move and play every day. The recommendations of the chief medical officers (DH, 2011) are that babies should be able to move freely in safe spaces and be on their tummies every day, while under-fives who are walking independently should be physically active for at least three hours a day (see Chapter 2 for more details of these recommendations). Practitioners and parents and carers need to talk to each other as often as possible about the children's movement-play and physical experiences at the setting and at home to ensure that they achieve the recommended levels of activity. Children need unstructured and imaginative play for opportunities to explore, be curious and make sense of the world around them.

The setting can find out about all the local green spaces and playgrounds available in the local area and provide a map with information for families about where they are and how to get there. For wet days, families may appreciate knowing about indoor facilities available locally, such as ball pools, soft play, swimming pools and gym clubs, as well as their cost and whether or not there are reductions for children under five years of age. Whatever the weather, infants and young children need to be outdoors every day, so settings can encourage parents to provide their children with wet weather clothes so they can play outside if it rains and warmer clothes and boots if it snows or is cold.

Days out at the weekend and holidays provide children with very valuable experiences to share with their parents, siblings, grandparents, aunts, uncles or friends. Parents and carers may take their children on a train ride to walk in a forest or the countryside or to swim in the sea and play in the sand. They will have space in these places to be more physically active than usual in a healthy environment, encouraging imaginative play. Make a special time together as a family or meet up with friends to go for a walk or play games together outdoors.

As we have seen, active play has benefits for children's physical development, their mental health and learning. Being sedentary while strapped in a car seat or pushchair should be minimised. There are times each day, however, that infants and young children benefit from being still and enjoying a quiet and peaceful time, when they might want to snuggle up for a cuddle or listen to or read a story. These are times when there should be no other distractions such as the television. These quiet times can help to calm infants and young children and bring them to the stillness that is also needed for their well-being.

Conclusion

For all older children to have a chance of being fit and healthy, we must address the importance of physical movement activities for them from birth and when very young. This area of children's development must start early in their childhood if they are to be developmentally and physically ready for formal education by the time they transition to school. Parents and carers therefore play a crucial role in their children's future heath, well-being and development.

Settings wanting to build effective partnerships with parents and carers must make home visits, where possible. These visits are crucial for establishing good relationships with parents and carers and gaining their commitment. Further, movement-play needs to be part of the conversation professionals have with parents. For all children to achieve their full potential, the quality of the HLE needs to be influenced by talking to parents about the ways in which they can encourage children to be physically active, especially outdoors. To be effective in bringing this about, however, all professionals need to receive training in movement-play from experienced tutors.

Every child deserves the best possible chance of reaching his or her full potential. Resilience appears to play an important part in the outcome for those at risk of underachievement. Two areas of resilience have been identified that can counter risks to young children: parental interest and involvement; and an enhanced and stimulating early HLE. Both of these areas rely on professionals developing effective partnerships with parents, so it can be seen just how essential this process is in order to give every child the best possible chance of succeeding and breaking the cycle of disadvantage.

Further reading

Goddard Blythe, S. (2008) *What Babies and Children Really Need*. Stroud: Hawthorn Press.

Mackett, R. (2004) 'Making children's lives more active'. London: Centre for Transport Studies, University College London.

Mackett, R.L. and Paskins, J. (2008) 'Children's physical activity: The contribution of playing and walking'. *Children & Society*, 22: 345–57. Paper supplied by author.

Pachter, L.M. and Dumont-Mathieu, T. (2004) 'Parenting in culturally divergent settings'. In M. Hoghughi and N. Long (eds), *Handbook of Parenting: Theory and research for practice*. London: Sage.

Play England (2011) 'Save Children's Play' flyer and action pack. Available online at: www.playengland.org.uk/resources/save-children's-play-flyer.aspx

Rutter, M. (2006b) 'Implications of resilience concepts for scientific understanding'. *New York Academy of Sciences*, 1094: 1–12.

Siraj-Blatchford, I. and Siraj-Blatchford, J. (2009) 'Improving children's attainment through a better quality of family-based support for early learning', Early Years Research Review 2. London: Centre for Excellence and Outcomes in Children and Young People's Services (C4EO). Available online at: http://archive.c4eo.org.uk/themes/earlyyears/familybasedsupport/files/c4eo_family_based_support_kr_2.pdf

Sunderland, M. (2007) *What Every Parent Needs to Know: The remarkable effects of love, nurture and play on your child's development*. London: Dorling Kindersley.

Sylva, K., Melhuish, E., Sammons, P., Siraj-Blatchford, I., Taggart, B. and Elliot, K. (2004) 'The Effective Provision of Pre-school Education (EPPE) Project: Findings from pre-school to end of Key State 1'. Institute of Education, University of London, University of Oxford, Birkbeck, University of London, and Sure Start for the Department for Education and Skills. Nottingham: DfES Publications.

6
Leading and managing the implementation of movement-play from practice to policy: a whole setting approach

Introduction

Early childhood provision is indeed in a prime position to contribute significantly towards achieving the recommended physical activity levels for children from birth to six years of age. Programmes for physical movement activity in early childhood education are critical for young children's future life chances. The effective implementation of any such programme, however, relies on strength of leadership (Siraj-Blatchford and Manni, 2007).

Investing in physical activity through movement-play at the early childhood education level involves developing policy, committing to training and liaising with parents and carers and the wider community. An effective policy gives members of staff, parents and carers and the community clear guidance on a setting's vision and pedagogy in the drive towards raising standards for the children in its care. Effective implementation of a programme and sustaining best practice are associated with effective leadership. This chapter will outline some of the behaviours identified as effective for those in leadership positions, which will, in turn, be related to developing a policy, as outlined in the guidance below.

Leadership and management

A study carried out by Siraj-Blatchford and Manni (2007) explored the qualities of effective leadership in the early years sector (ELEYS) and it revealed the complexity that leaders are faced with today. Dunlop (2008: 4) draws our attention to the distinction between management and leadership found in the educational literature.

It is clear that managers and heads are confronted with managing many responsibilities, not least of which are the outcomes for children's learning and development, and all that this entails, while at the same time attempting to meet the growing demands related to administrative tasks, such as budgeting, managing adults, maintaining home–setting links, monitoring children's progress and keeping abreast of current nursery needs, to name but a few.

Leadership in early childhood education and care calls for a clear vision, based on shared values and setting standards, being able to motivate staff and provide them with direction (Dunlop, 2008: 5).

Leaders are therefore currently faced with numerous tasks associated with the demands of both management *and* leadership. In this chapter, we highlight the balance that leaders are striving to achieve in their attempt to reconcile these sometimes competing demands while implementing movement-play through a whole setting approach to developing policy.

Siraj-Blatchford and Manni (2007: 15) state that, 'the primary goal of any early childhood setting should be to improve (social and intellectual) educational outcomes'. Children's experiences and progress in early years education are undoubtedly of overriding importance to those in leadership positions. This is, after all, the raison d'être for the settings' existence – they are there for the children, their care and education – but how is this to be achieved?

Research into the effective provision of preschool education (EPPE) has shown that there is a link between children's outcomes and the quality of the provision, so high-quality care is associated with improved developmental outcomes for children and, conversely, lower-quality care with poorer outcomes (Belsky, 2001; Burchinal et al., 2000; Sylva et al., 2004). Also, children from disadvantaged backgrounds are considered to be the most affected by the quality of care (Melhuish, 2003).

Clearly, quality is crucial to young children's present and future development. The question is, therefore, what influences quality at an early childhood setting? Siraj-Blatchford and Manni (2007) in the ELEYS study found that the quality of a setting was influenced by the effectiveness of the leadership of that setting. In other words, 'effective leadership and management are central to the quality care agenda' (Dunlop, 2008: 15).

Examination of the types of leadership behaviours undertaken in effective early years settings has revealed that a commitment to collaboration and improving children's learning outcomes were key (Siraj and Hallet, 2014; Siraj-Blatchford and Manni, 2007).

Further categories of effective leadership practice are (Siraj-Blatchford and Manni, 2007: 26):

- identifying and articulating a collective vision with regard to pedagogy and curriculum
- ensuring shared understandings, meanings and goals – building common purposes
- effective communication
- encouraging reflection, which acts as an impetus for change
- commitment to ongoing professional development and supporting staff to become critically reflective of their practice
- monitoring and assessing practice, through a collaborative dialogue
- building a team culture and establishing a community of learners
- encouraging and facilitating parent and community partnerships, promoting achievement for all young children
- distributed leadership.

The above categories will be discussed, where applicable, under the headings below in the guidance that is given for writing a policy on physical development. Establishing comprehensive guidelines for physical development for early childhood provision should result in higher levels of physical activity and, consequently, healthier children.

The following advice and template were written by Lynn Linsell, Senior Manager at the Integrated Early Years Service, London Borough of Camden.

How to use the example template for writing a physical development policy

You can use this example template policy for early years settings in conjunction with this chapter, which gives guidance on writing a physical development policy in order to help you successfully develop and implement your own policy.

The information included in physical development policies varies. This template will help you to consider what information you would like to include in your setting's policy. The information included in the example template is in line with the national best practice guidance.

Read each heading in the example template and consider the short description in *italics*. The latter are example statements that you can either include or adapt for your own policy. If any of the headings are not relevant to your setting, these can be deleted. You can also personalise the example template policy by inserting your setting's logo (in the header) and name (in the title).

[Insert name of your setting]'s physical development policy

General information

Name of setting:

Name of member of staff responsible for the physical development policy:

Date of implementation of policy:

Introduction

In this section, outline the importance of physical activity and movement in the early years and the impact they have on all areas of children's development and learning.

Aim of the policy

Explain here what the setting aims to achieve through the policy. For example, 'To increase the activity level of children and families who attend the centre through the provision of a supportive environment conducive to physical activity.'

Mission statement/rationale

Explain how your overall aims link to the requirements of the Statutory Framework for the Early Years Foundation Stage (EYFS), Every Child Matters and other local or national policies and frameworks. For example, cover the importance of providing opportunities for young children to be active and interact, and develop their coordination, control and movement, and helping children to understand the importance of physical activity and movement.

Development and implementation of the physical activity policy

In this section, describe how you have developed/are going to develop the policy – for example, how you have engaged with staff, parents, carers and children.
In this section, also explain:

- *how you will implement the policy in the setting – how it will be shared with staff, parents and carers, for example*
- *how you plan to promote the policy and ensure that everyone it applies to is aware of it – displaying it on the noticeboard, placing it on the website and so on.*

(Continued)

(Continued)

Communicating with children and families

Use this section to describe how you communicate with children and families about physical activity, the health benefits and different activities taking place at the centre and in the area. It is also important to communicate with parents and carers about their children's individual needs.

Equal opportunities

All children at the centre, including those with special needs, are entitled to a comprehensive programme of physical activity that allows every child to improve their skills and develop positive attitudes towards physical activities, including sport.

Use this section to outline how you will ensure the inclusion of all children in physical activity.

Physical activity at the centre

It is important that a variety of structured and unstructured physical activities are planned for both walkers and non-walkers and they are suitable for the different stages of children's development.

In this section, explain what activities are planned at the centre, what opportunities there are for physical activity and movement and how staff encourage activity and engage with the children.

Explain how the activities on offer support children's development and are in line with the revised EYFS Framework.

Supportive environment

Explain the steps your centre takes to ensure that the environment, both inside and outside, promotes physical activity. Things to consider include:

- *specific equipment, playground markings*
- *the process for carrying out risk assessments and managing risk*
- *the procedure for off-site visits to take part in physical activity in the community.*

Involving families

It is important that families are encouraged to take part in physical activities in the centre with their children and on their own and accurate information is provided to families on the national recommendations for physical activity.

Use this section to describe what activities are available and how they are promoted to families to encourage them to attend. Outline how physical activity guidelines are provided to families.

Active travel

Active travel is a simple, low-cost and effective way to incorporate physical activity into individuals' lives. Active travel includes walking, cycling, scootering and skateboarding.

Use this section to describe how you encourage families to use active means to travel to and from the centre and any facilities you provide to ensure scooters and bikes can be parked safely.

Sessions for staff

It is important that high-quality learning opportunities are available to members of staff to ensure that they are kept up to date with the most relevant activities for child development.

It is also important for them to be encouraged to take part in physical activity themselves.

Use this section to explain what training or professional development opportunities there are for staff and if physical activity sessions are promoted or run for staff at the centre.

Linked policies/guidelines

List all relevant policies and guidelines.

Evaluation and review of the setting's approach to physical development

It is important to evaluate and reflect on everything you do within your setting, including your approach to physical activity. Use this section to outline how you plan to evaluate your approach to physical activity throughout the setting and review the policy. Consider:

- *getting feedback from parents, carers and the children*
- *looking at the ways other settings in your area approach physical activity*
- *feedback from staff who attend training*
- *assessing your setting's progress in using the MPS (see Chapter 4), reviewing the physical activity policy at least once a year in consultation with children and their families*
- *auditing and reviewing resources.*

Date for policy review:
Signed:
Date:

A guide to writing a physical development policy

In Chapter 1, evidence was cited for the influence that movement activities have on young children's learning and development. Subsequently, Chapter 2 emphasised the possible health benefits for young children in relation to increased physical activity levels. This knowledge and information may suggest changes you want to make to current practices at a setting level in relation to physical activity. Basing changes at a setting level on evidence from research is likely to be better received than expecting staff to change practices just for the sake of it.

A key area of leadership revealed in the 'Researching effective pedagogy in the early years' (REPEY) report (Siraj-Blatchford et al., 2002) is that which promotes evidence-based practice. Leaders willing to embrace evidence-based practice at their settings provided a solid foundation on which to promote confidence and convince members of staff to accept change.

Those in leadership positions might therefore find starting with research-based evidence useful in evaluating the need for change in their provision. Earlier chapters in this book have provided guidance on the practical application of physical movement activities in early years settings. Also, research has been mentioned throughout and in what follows when findings have been useful in relation to a pedagogical application, with the aim of supporting practitioners in the challenges they may face in the implementation of this work with children.

This policy guidance is intended to support settings in establishing best practice throughout the provision in order that children are provided with a wealth of physical movement activities to help them to be healthy and reach their full potential. It can be adapted to ensure that the policy reflects the needs and character of any setting. A number of headings are listed that you might like to use to structure your own policy.

Rationale

The rationale for writing a policy will be based at any particular time on national and local priorities and the latest research. These should underpin the key characteristics of a policy document and provide the impetus for producing an effective one.

Here are some aspects to consider.

- The beliefs and values held at the setting that will shape your policy. Strong emphasis should be placed on an inclusive approach to provision and practice to ensure equality of opportunities for all the children.
- The influence that specific movement activities have on children's development of coordination, posture, movement and the brain.
- The rationale for a physical development policy that, ideally, will be linked to all areas of the curriculum or domains of children's development (see Chapter 1 for more details).
- That all areas within and outside the setting where physical activities take place will be identified.
- National and/or local statistics about obesity.
- Any local initiatives related to obesity, such as a strategic policy on improving health outcomes for families and young children. An effective policy will have regard for a borough or county-wide approach to the health and well-being of all young children (see Chapter 5 for an example of one borough's healthy lifestyles project).
- Regarding nutrition, that the food and drink provided should include adequate nutrients across a range of meals. See guidance from the Children's Food Trust (formerly the School Food Trust) and the Caroline Walker Trust, mentioned in Chapter 2.

Reflective practice

Consider whether or not your policy promotes an evidence-based health and developmental message to staff, parents, carers and management committees.

Please see the chief medical officers' physical activity guidelines for children under five years of age in Chapter 2 as these are relevant to all children, whatever their gender, race or socio-economic status (DH, 2011).

The purpose

The purpose of writing a policy is to ensure that all members of staff, children, parents and carers and the wider community are not only aware of the whole setting's approach to physical development but also effectively implement it consistently throughout. An effective leader ensures that there is consistency of understanding of practices and processes by members of staff (Siraj-Blatchford and Manni, 2007).

The benefits of physical activity for young children's health, learning and development can be disseminated to the staff, children, parents and carers and management committees. The methods chosen to disseminate this vital information may determine its success so will need to be given some thought, but training, support and advice have been shown to be particularly effective means of disseminating this information within early childhood education provision (Archer and Siraj, 2015; see also Chapter 4 for more information).

Principles

- The setting's commitment to free-flow play indoors and outdoors. If free-flow play is not possible, then a statement can be included in the policy regarding how all the children will access opportunities to be physically active each day. Levels of physical activity should be in line with the chief medical officers' recommendations.
- The importance of children enjoying energetic physical activity indoors and out and the feeling of well-being that comes from that experience.
- The need for physical activity to be inclusive for all (including staff!).
- That the physical activities offered are appropriate for every child's development so children can explore their own body movement potential.
- Positive attitudes about being physically active to be shared by all staff. The head might consider new staff members' attitudes to physical activity when they join the setting and discuss the details of the setting's policy with them.

Staff act as good role models by appreciating the importance of physical activity, good nutrition and engaging in these with the children.

Some questions to consider

- Have you shared the principles with parents and carers? Parents may wish to add more or develop them further. How will you involve them in this process?

- Do staff follow the guidelines recommended by the chief medical officers, that adults should be active for 150 minutes a week?
- What provision is made for staff and children to actively travel to and from the setting? If children cycle or scooter to the setting, where can they store bikes or scooters? If staff run to work, are there facilities for refreshing and changing?

The process

The process of developing a policy is paramount if any change is to be effectively implemented. Siraj-Blatchford and Manni (2007: 17) point out that, 'change is best seen as a process rather than an event' and 'management of the process will largely effect the success or failure of the implemented change'. Changing ways of working, however, is not an easy task and some members of staff may find the implementation of new aims and goals quite challenging, a challenge that they may or may not rise to. Effective leaders, therefore, need to have the 'capacity to influence others into action' and lead them (Siraj-Blatchford and Manni, 2007: 16).

To achieve this, effective leaders will be reflective practitioners themselves and encourage reflective practice in others (Siraj and Hallet, 2014; Siraj-Blatchford and Manni, 2007). Reflecting with members of staff about current practice and consulting them about change will support the process of change. This process also demands that leaders communicate with them as well as promote effective communication between all members of staff. The promotion of a collective ethos in the setting will support everyone so that they work consistently with the children and families.

Figure 6.1 outlines the steps that should be taken in the process of developing an effective policy and each of these steps is described in detail below.

Effective leadership and management

When developing a whole-setting approach to policy, effective leadership is crucial if it is to have the maximum impact. A key feature of effective leadership identified in the ELEYS study is the ability to 'inspire others with a vision of a better future' (Siraj-Blatchford and Manni, 2007: 16). Effective leaders are able to identify a vision for the setting and, through discussions with members of staff, co-construct shared objectives to realise that vision. In this way, effective leaders

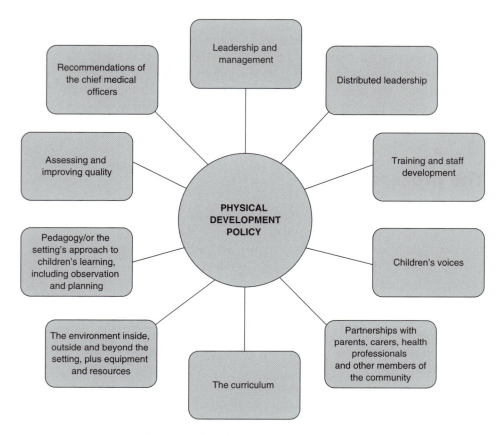

Figure 6.1 *Factors that need to be considered and decided on when drawing up a physical development policy*

begin the process of promoting a shared understanding with all those working at the setting in order to ensure consistency, especially in relation to pedagogy and the curriculum.

Aspects for consideration include the following:

- Writing the policy should begin with considering current practice to give all those concerned an opportunity to shape new aspects. Starting with present practice in nutrition and physical activity will value what staff currently do and acknowledge the importance of the opportunities already provided for the children.
- Find out how confident members of staff feel in this particular curriculum area and establish any training requirements.
- Carry out an audit to establish which resources and equipment are presently in place that enable children to be physically active.
- Make it clear from the outset that the intention is to promote physical development through movement-play throughout the setting.

- Plan together with the members of staff how the whole setting can achieve this intention.
- Heads, managers and deputies need to agree to committing to invest in training for physical development through movement-play and join members of staff in any training. Access training locally from early years advisory staff.
- Follow the chief medical officers' recommendations regarding levels of physical activity for young children outlined in their guidance (see Chapter 2).
- Establish how active travel can be promoted at the setting for children, parents and staff (see Chapter 5).
- Lead discussions on the principles that the setting chooses to adopt for children's physical development. These may include the four guiding principles of the Statutory Framework for the EYFS: a unique child, positive relationships, enabling environments and children learning and developing in different ways and at different rates.
- Access training locally, too, from your Health Improvement Team on Healthy Eating. Does your setting follow the Children's Food Trust (2012) or the Caroline Walker Trust's guidelines (2006)?

The above points should help clarify the intentions and goals you are attempting to achieve and enable everyone to understand and be inspired by what it is they are working together to make this a reality for the children.

> Has the setting accessed training locally for movement-play and healthy eating?

Distributed leadership

The ELEYS study revealed that leadership in early childhood settings is not now viewed as the responsibility of a single person, but, instead, a variety of people will be responsible for contributing to effective leadership. In this way, leadership is distributed (Siraj-Blatchford and Manni, 2007: 21).

Effective leaders distribute tasks to members of staff because, in their ever-demanding and complex role, they cannot possibly do everything themselves. There are different ways of achieving this. Effective leaders recognise the potential strengths of all staff in the setting and so may identify someone they consider capable of taking on the responsibility of coordinating, monitoring progress and overseeing the implementation of the policy for physical development. Alternatively, a staff member may volunteer to take on this responsibility. Whichever is the case, 'managers of effective settings show a clear recognition' that staff who take on new leadership responsibilities need 'support to develop the skills required to meet these new demands' (Siraj-Blatchford and Manni, 2007: 21).

Building a team culture of responsibility will necessitate that a link person also be identified in each room of the early childhood setting to feed back relevant information to the lead person. So, strong links need to be made between all members of staff who are involved or who have a specific interest in physical activity, including movement-play. In this way, the setting promotes a collaborative learning environment in which effective leaders play a key role (Siraj-Blatchford and Manni, 2007: 22).

Training and development

The ELEYS study highlighted effective leaders as showing a commitment to the ongoing professional developmental needs of the staff. To fulfil this commitment, members of staff will need to attend courses and access reading materials, such as relevant books, academic papers and educational journals, to become more critically reflective in their practice.

Effective leaders not only support and encourage critically reflective practice in others, but are also reflective practitioners themselves (Siraj-Blatchford and Manni, 2007). Leaders therefore need to consider:

- how staff development needs are identified and fulfilled
- how staff who are not confident in this area will be supported at the setting
- what induction procedures will be in place for new members of staff
- how to identify training opportunities for those taking lead roles in this curriculum area
- the continuing professional development needs of all staff on an ongoing basis, such as training, coaching, mentoring
- the need for staff to engage with children in their physical movement activities
- the timescale for identifying the overall needs of the setting, writing the policy and implementating it.

Children's voices

Pascal and Bertram (2009) are committed to children's participation and have searched for ways to effectively listen to and work alongside children in order to explore and document their experiences of early childhood settings. They believe that as researchers they must become experts in listening to children and familiar with the ways in which children communicate with them. In recognition of the work carried out in this field which promotes children's perspectives Clark and Moss (2005) constructed a wide-ranging picture of suggested practices for listening to young children known as the Mosaic Approach. The following ideas are ways in which children can be truly listened to and their views be taken into account. These have come from *Listening to Young Children: The Mosaic Approach* (Clark and Moss, 2011: 4), which promotes practices that consult with children in an attempt to co-construct meaning together.

- Children can use cameras, draw, make books, use drama, puppetry and tours, and make maps to enable them to express their thoughts and observations and so participate in the process of co-construction.
- Adults can listen to the child or children and engage in interpreting, constructing meaning and responding in such a way that, together, they reflect on the children's perspective (Clark and Moss, 2011).
- By talking with children, practitioners can gain more knowledge about their experiences of movement activities. This is not limited to the spoken word, however, and should include babies' responses by observing what they say 'through their play, their actions and reactions' (Clark and Moss, 2011: 7).

In these participatory ways, the children can let their parents or practitioners know their views on and experiences of the movement activities at the setting. This insightful knowledge of the children's perspective will support staff assessing the provision and planning appropriately for individual children. In this way, children's voices contribute to the development of the policy.

Partnerships with parents, carers and the wider community

Early childhood leadership in effective settings places a strong emphasis on working in partnership with parents (Sylva et al., 2004). The EPPE research (Sylva et al., 2004) showed that parental support in the HLE influences young children's outcomes. As noted earlier, it is what parents *do* with their children at home that is important, so the most effective settings provide 'pedagogic and parental support in the provision of an effective home learning environment' (Siraj-Blatchford and Manni, 2007: 14). With this insight, effective leaders encourage and facilitate parent partnerships, thus promoting consistency across home and setting in relation to the children's nutrition and physical movement experiences.

Parents and carers are the critical link between the setting and home, ensuring the children have a broad range of physical experiences. When communicating with parents, it is important to be aware of the complexity of some family structures today and the diversity of family units (this diversity and parent partnerships are discussed in more detail in Chapters 2 and 5 respectively). The relationship between the early childhood setting and parents and carers is critical to the promotion of young children's health, well-being, learning and development. This relationship is likely to begin more effectively when home visits are enshrined in the setting's policy. Chapter 5 discusses the importance of home visits and influencing the HLE with regard to children's early movement patterns and physical activity.

Here are some aspects to consider:

- Parents informing the setting about their children's interests and achievements in relation to movement-play, detailing behaviour and social development. Parents and staff exchange information about what new physical activities the children are experiencing and their achievements. This exchange can offer 'consistency of learning opportunities between home and setting' (Siraj-Blatchford and Manni, 2007: 24). See Chapter 5 for an example of how one setting gathers information from parents about their children's physical activities at home.
- Including parents at staff training days. By actively encouraging them to participate, by attending courses the setting has planned, for example, parents become conscious of their influential role in their children's development. This is likely to 'improve the quality of their interactions with their children and improve the learning activities that they provide' (Siraj-Blatchford and Manni, 2007: 23).
- Holding separate training sessions for parents on nutrition and/or physical development through movement-play.
- Holding parents meetings about the influence of movement-play on children's health, learning and development, at various times of the day, in order to reach as many parents as possible.
- Inviting parents into the setting to see the children and adults engaging in movement-play activities and to join in if they feel confident about doing so. Staff can then take this opportunity to talk to parents and carers about the links to learning and development, health and well-being.
- Displaying photos and drawings of children at the setting and at home in a variety of physical activities and movement patterns.
- Showing a film about the link between physical activity and brain development and/or about children moving. (Contact the authors of

this book for free copies of the short DVD *Moving, Learning and Growing: The role of movement in child play and development.*)

- Giving fathers a focus for these meetings, such as more outdoor activities.
- Inviting families to join their children on a sponsored walk in your local park to raise money for any resources that are needed.
- Loaning bags of resources to parents to take home and use in movement activities with their children.

Reflective practice

Is home visiting part of the setting's policy? If this is not possible, what is in place instead for gathering important information about children and their histories of early movement patterns and their interests in physical activity?

Have parents and carers been included in decisionmaking and policy issues at the setting in this crucial area of their child's development? See Chapter 5 for more details of ways in which to encourage parents and carers to become involved and keep them involved.

Has the setting advised parents and carers about how they can build physical activities into their children's daily routines, such as walking or cycling rather than travelling by car each day?

Has the setting linked up with other health professionals, such as health visitors, occupational therapists, physiotherapists, the health improvement team, or any other community and charitable organisations, such as Learning through Landscapes, the Woodland Trust, the Royal Society for the Protection of Birds and the Royal Horticultural Society, which can advise on access to outdoor spaces for children to be physically active or places where children can be in touch with the natural world?

The curriculum

An effective leader will collaborate with the staff to develop a collective vision with regard to the curriculum. One of the key leadership responsibilities is to support and improve children's learning and development, so effective leaders will focus their attention on teaching and learning.

In the context of physical development, this would involve monitoring and assessing practice and the environment. The most successful managers in the ELEYS study recognised the 'importance of adult–child interactions and supported staff in developing better ways of engaging children' (Siraj-Blatchford and Manni, 2007: 16). It is through adult engagement in movement activities with children that the quality of children's physical movement experiences can be enhanced (Archer and Siraj, 2015), which, in turn, will have a direct effect on their development.

Children are likely to make better progress in settings where adults plan movement experiences according to the needs of each individual child. Monitoring and assessing practice through a collaborative dialogue is an important part of the process of improving quality and, consequently, children's outcomes.

CASE STUDY

We observed a group of preschool children in our study (Archer and Siraj, 2015) who were provided with mats and large soft shapes. They chose to climb on to the cubes and jump onto the mats.

Two of the boys weren't so pleased with the jumps they could achieve with the arrangement of the resources as it was, so they continually reorganised the items until they realised their idea of the perfect leap. In this way, they were able to solve their own problems through body and mind experiential learning.

As children ask questions, experiment, design and solve problems, they begin to gain knowledge of the world they live in. Young children learn to cooperate with others as they move together and share space and resources. These physical experiences develop in children an increasing control of their gross and fine motor movements.

Movement experiences for young children are integral to all areas of the curriculum. For example, when infants and children use their bodies to express their delight, needs, ideas and feelings, they engage with their creativity. Running, jumping, skipping, climbing and balancing can be expressed mathematically, as they judge how high they can jump or climb and estimate distances when balancing or walking along a plank, for example.

The environment, indoors and outdoors

Enabling environments is one aspect of the EYFS curriculum. The setting's physical development policy should include examples that illustrate how its environment will support and value physical activity indoors and outdoors.

Please refer once more to Item 1: Space and resources of the MPS in Chapter 4, which can be used to assess and improve the environment. You will recall that sufficient floor space needs to be available indoors for the children to be physically active in a variety of ways, such as tummy time, crawling, climbing, spinning and rough and tumble. Resources, where possible, need be accessible for children to engage in different levels of physical activity, including physically demanding play. (For a comprehensive list of resources, see the Notes for clarification for Item 1 of the MPS.) If followed, the range of activities provided and the organisation of the environment will enable children to spontaneously participate in physical movement activities alone or with their peers and adults.

The outdoors provides a non-threatening context for infants and young children to learn about their world. Children need an outside environment with natural stimuli that will inspire them to learn and enjoy physical challenges as they create dens from ropes, branches and materials, using their creativity and imagination with open-ended resources. 'Outdoors' includes gardens, playgrounds, parks, adventure playgrounds and fields, for example.

Adventurous and vigorous physical activity stimulates the neurological system, develops young children's ability to take risks and improves their confidence and health. Being outdoors affords children the opportunity to develop a sense of freedom and movement and be creative, messy and make noise on a larger scale than may be possible indoors. Early childhood settings, therefore, need to provide a range of flexible resources that will encourage movement through creativity, such as sheets of paper, paints and rollers for mark-making and painting on a large scale, or musical instruments, scarves and ribbons to encourage creative movement or a range of guttering and pipes to explore water. Resources that are in kit form for children to put together will help to make the most of spontaneous activities.

Importantly, young children need to be supported outdoors by enthusiastic adults who will join in with learning opportunities and co-play rather than just passively observe. Take time to ensure risk assessments are effective and robust and that play opportunities for young children are safe and suitable, but still offer challenge and develop a sense of independence. The key is not to eliminate risk but to weigh up the perceived risks and hazards against the play benefits.

Aspects to consider include:

- modifications that need to be made to ensure all children have equal access to physical activities
- whether or not the children consider the environments playful or restrictive
- environments that offer children opportunities to play outdoors each day
- access to natural environments, with trees to climb, grassy slopes to roll down, mud to dig and logs for balancing, for example

- allowing children to take their shoes and socks off to feel the sensations of different surfaces indoors and outdoors, such as splashing in water and squelching in mud, and babies like to play with their toes, too, pushing themselves off with them as they tummy crawl, then, eventually, standing up on their bare feet, balancing perfectly.

Equipment and resources

The setting will need to identify the following:

- An annual budget to continue to further physical development.
- A person responsible for identifying needs, monitoring resources and maintaining them.
- Resources to purchase for movement activities indoors.
- Equipment to purchase that encourages more challenging physical experiences outdoors, such as climbing frames and slides, a tree house, a climbing wall, wheelbarrows, reclaimed bricks, sand and water, ladders and ropes, monkey bars, A-frames and ladders, balancing equipment, spinning cones and resource kits. Think about what you like the children to be able to do out of doors rather than what you would like them to have to ensure items have both a play and money value. Consider the different ways in which physical development can be afforded through loose, flexible resources, as well as fixed equipment.
- Natural environments for children, with trees to climb, grassy slopes and hills to roll down, mud to dig, places for planting vegetables to eat, herbs for cooking, flowers to grow from seeds and bulbs, logs and fallen trees.
- Places for children to be still and quiet both indoors and outdoors.

Pedagogy or the setting's approach to children's learning

Research has shown that the role of the adult makes a difference to children's outcomes. The adult's role is central to children's engagement in physical movement activity in terms of their participation, the intensity of the activities they engage in and how long they spend being physically active.

Vygostsky (Daniels, 2001) highlights the importance of the adult in assisting children in their playful exploration, which, ultimately, leads to them extending and enhancing their learning. Please refer to Item 2:

Adults engaging in movement with the children of the MPS (Chapter 4) for guidance on progression in this area.

Adults are also responsible for observation, assessment and planning. Here are some spects to consider:

- Are all members of staff confident about observing, assessing and planning children's participation in physical movement activities?
- Does the two-year-old progress check include the child's early movement patterns, such as floor play, rolling from back to tummy and vice versa, tummy time and crawling on all fours, all of which take place prior to walking?
- How do you ensure that parents and carers contribute to the children's nutritional and physical development assessment?
- How are children's and parents' views gathered and acted on?
- Are children's individual interests in physical activities and their schemas identified and planned for?
- Has each child been observed engaging in physical activity for the duration recommended by the chief medical officers?
- Have all children been observed using both indoor and outdoor environments when engaged in physical experiences?

Has the early childhood setting decided on a method for recording children's physical development over time, such as collecting ongoing evidence for each child that may be presented in their portfolios or learning journey folders? How is this information translated into planning for the children? Please refer to Item 3: Planning for movement-play from observations of the children of the MPS (Chapter 4) for guidance on progression in this area.

An example of one setting's planning sheet can be seen in Table 6.1.

Aspects to consider

- What resources are already in place?
- What resources and equipment are needed that can be found or bought or donated by families?
- Consult other professionals for their advice about provision, such as movement specialists, occupational therapists and physiotherapists.
- Whether or not free-flow play is operating at your setting, so that infants and young children can move from indoors to outside and vice versa at will.
- If free-flow play is not possible, how is your setting providing opportunities for children to play outside each day?

Table 6.1 *Example of a planning sheet for physical development*

Big gym sessions: physical development sessions

Days 28 July	Session times and title	Developmental areas	Equipment needed	Targeted areas for specific children
Monday	Yoga, big room. Soft play, small room Afternoon – playing with bats and balls.	Focusing on task and becoming aware of their bodies and their capabilities. Spatial awareness. Developing hand–eye coordination skills using bats.	Yoga teacher, Claire. Soft play room.	Adult support in soft play for H. and AA. Adult support for AR in big room to access yoga.
Tuesday	Dance 10–11. Big gym 3–4.30	Following guidance, becoming aware of body. Using body to express. Moving rhythmically. Becoming breathless. Dance. Big gym – balance skills and fluidity of movement.	Big gym – need the wooden beams and blocks, tunnel and rhythm sticks, plus a frame and hoops. Nisha and Gemma to set up.	Ask A to concentrate on hopping and moving from side to side for AA. Big gym – set up obstacle course, concentrating on balancing skills and fluid movements for FL and ES. AA and H need adult support throughout.
Weds	Garden session. Using garden tools to dig and rake and sweep. Using wagons for pulling heavy loads. Riding balance bikes. Rolling down hill.	Using hand–eye coordination for tools. Using muscles to dig and move heavy loads. Using different areas of body to dig, move, rake and sweep.	Wagons, tools, mud digging area. Have available throughout the day. Balance bikes with helmets. Supervise.	Balance bikes for ES as cautious and needs to develop skills. Supervise garden tools and safe use. Remind some children of safe use.
Thurs	All large equipment out for free choice.	Concentrate on climbing wall.	Climbing wall and all large play equipment.	Adult at site.

Days 28 July	Session times and title	Developmental areas	Equipment needed	Targeted areas for specific children
Friday	Big gym 3–4.30	Music session – dance and games to music. Use balls and ribbons to move gracefully. Adult-led and child-led.	Adults, music, ribbon sticks, balls.	Build FL's confidence to move and choose what to do.
Notes			Big gym ideas. Walk along a beam, weave in and out of cones, holding a ball, try to lift up and down from squatting. Throw and catch a ball Bears walking in different directions, hopping on one leg. Follow the leader. Musical statues. Spinning. Rolling. Obstacle course. Sweeping. Races – three-legged, commando, egg and spoon. Squats. Jumping back and forwards. Tiger walk. Climbing. Dancing to music. A-frame, swinging and hanging.	Equipment: tunnel balls (all sizes) bats, hockey sticks, racquets etc. hoops ribbons ball with bells wooden beams wooden blocks spin chair spades, forks and other garden tools brooms hill trees for climbing rope for making rope ladders A-frames climbing wall pull-along wagons balance bikes

Source: Collingham Gardens Nursery

Assessing and improving quality in movement-play – the MPS

The MPS is useful for measuring progress in implementing movement-play at settings for all ages from birth to early primary school and is available in Chapter 4.

Consideration should be given to who will take responsibility for initially administering the MPS, so that an assessment can be made of the setting's starting point and, from there, plan progression. The scale is useful on an ongoing basis to support staff in developing and improving quality in this area of the curriculum.

The recommendations of the chief medical officers for physical activity for children from birth to five years of age can be found in the following boxes.

From birth, not yet walking unaided

The consensus between the health officials and movement specialists Lamont and Goddard Blythe is clear: specific movement activities are central to a baby's growth and development. For those children who cannot yet walk, it is essential to provide space for them to be on their backs and tummies, to kick their legs and move their arms, crawl, play and roll around on the floor and pull up to standing from the months immediately following birth until they are walking confidently. Water-based activities for parents or carers and babies are also recommended.

Infants not yet walking need space to play wearing unrestrictive clothing to enable them to move their legs and arms, reach for and grasp objects, turn their heads towards stimuli, pull and push and play with other people. Space needs to be uncluttered for infants to move while objects are just out of reach to encourage them to move and roll over towards them.

Infants who are reluctant movers need to feel the rhythm of movement in their bodies as trusted adults hold them in their arms while they spin and dance or safely toss them in the air.

All this development takes time and infants need to rehearse these movements repeatedly until they are capable and competent movers.

Preschool children walking unaided

The minimum amount of time recommended by the chief medical officers for daily physical activity for preschool children walking unaided is 180 minutes (3 hours). This should not to be taken all at the same time, but spread throughout the day. Young children need to be physically active on a regular basis, however, for more time than this to benefit from additional health gains. A gradual increase in physical activity is recommended for children under five years old who are very inactive.

Young children emerging from floor-based play to walking unaided require unstructured, active and energetic play. These children will need to be active several hours a day to develop their fundamental movement skills and master their physical environment. Indeed, new physical activity guidelines recommend that children have the 'freedom to create their own opportunities for active play, direct their own play and engage in imaginative play' (DH, 2011: 22). Similarly, optimal early years practice is based on sound principles of play and active learning, putting the child at the heart of practice.

For the toddler who is up and about, climbing equipment indoors and out is essential, such as ladders, slides and bridges, as well as soft play shapes, tunnels for crawling through, earth to dig and cones to spin in.

Regular physical activity will promote the development of motor skills and healthy weight, enhance bone and muscular development, and support children's learning, behaviour and social skills.

The consequences of *reduced* physical activity, however, are low skill levels and low movement competence, which are a major barrier to participation in sport later in life. Furthermore, children with low motor competence tend to be active less often, spend less time playing and interacting with their peers, and play less on playground equipment. This is further evidence that movement skills are vital for children's learning and development and a 'lack of confidence and competence in performing these skills can have detrimental effects on children's social and emotional well-being' (Evangelou et al., 2009: 72).

Sedentary behaviour engaged in for long periods of time reduces opportunities for young children to be physically active. As noted, reduced physical activity is detrimental to their health and their natural tendencies to be active (DH, 2011: 27). More energetic activities that make children huff and puff will encourage development of their cardiorespiratory system (DH, 2011: 26). Young children therefore need to be physically active over the course of the day and, at times, engaged in more energetic activities, such as those listed in the boxes.

Active play

Active play should encourage young children to:

- use their large muscle groups
- practise a wide range of different movements
- experience a variety of play spaces and equipment
- set up their own play areas
- make up their own active play
- have fun and feel good about themselves and what they can do.

Under fives should also benefit from walking/skipping to and from the setting, shops, a friend's home or park (DH, 2011).

More energetic active play activities

- Climbing
- Running and chasing games
- Jumping
- Hopping
- Skipping
- Swinging
- Hanging upside down
- Hanging from monkey bars
- Balancing
- Riding

- Kicking balls
- Throwing and catching
- Rolling
- Rough and tumble
- Dancing
- Gymnastics
- Playing games in the park
- Riding a bike
- Water-based activities

(DH, 2011)

Settings may wish to include a statement in their policy about how the health and learning requirements in the EYFS will be met, so that all staff have a shared understanding of the most effective practice. Promoting and developing shared aims and objectives consistently with all staff were seen as crucial in the most effective settings identified in the ELEYS (Siraj-Blatchford and Manni, 2007).

Aspects for consideration include:

- an exploration of how movement-play links across all areas of the curriculum, so that members of staff can understand how young children use their bodies in all areas of their learning

- an outline of physical activities through movement-play for all age groups in the policy
- actions to be taken to ensure that all children are included.

How will the setting ensure that the chief medical officers' (DH, 2011) recommendations for levels of physical activity are met for *all* children?

Figure 6.2 *Example of a physical development policy*

Physical Development Policy

Regents Park Children's Centre

Name of staff member responsible for physical development policy:

Sue Williamson/Sharon Donovan.

Date of policy implementation: November 2014

Introduction

Physical Development is one of the three areas together with Personal and Social Development and Communication and Language that the **Early Years Foundation Stage (EYFS)** term as the prime areas of learning. The EYFS states that the prime areas "reflect the key skills and capacities all children need to develop and learn effectively, and become ready for school."

Aim of the policy

To increase the activity level of children and families who attend the Centre, through the provision of a supportive environment conducive to physical activity.

Rationale

The overall aims of this policy link directly with Section 1 (The Learning and Development Requirements) of the **EYFS**, specifically **1.6 Physical development** which:

"...involves providing opportunities for young children to be active and interactive; and to develop their co-ordination, control, and movement. Children must also be helped to

(Continued)

(Continued)

*understand the importance of physical activity, and to make
healthy choices in relation to food. "*

This also links to national targets to reduce childhood obesity.

Development and implementation of the physical activity policy

This policy has been developed in line with the model policy used as
part of the Little Steps to Healthy Lives Programme and with the
support of the Children Centre's Development Managers and the
EYFS Manager.

The policy will be shared with staff, parents and carers.
Periodically ways will be found to capture the views and responses
of the children.

A copy of the policy will be made available to all parents as part
of their induction.

Communicating with children and families

The Centre communicates with families about physical activity by:

- Discussing children's individual needs during the home visit, open
  day, settling in period and review meetings.
- Communicating events to parents via newsletters, text messages,
  posters etc.
- Involving parents in events such as sports days, open days, workshops and exercise classes.
- Using displays to promote all aspects of healthy development.

We communicate with children through:

- Curriculum activities
- Books and stories
- Role Play
- Music and movement sessions
- Indoor and outdoor physical play
- Forest school sessions
- Sports Day
- Open day

Equal Opportunity

All children at the Centre, including those with special needs, are entitled to a comprehensive programme of physical activity which allows everyone to improve their skills and develop positive attitudes towards physical activities including sports. We ensure the inclusion of all children in physical activity by:

- Differentiating and adapting curriculum activities to meet all children's individual needs.
- Children with specific disabilities having individual exercise programmes drawn up with their physiotherapist or occupational therapist as part of their Individual Education Plan (IEP).
- Children receiving 1-1 support if appropriate.
- Children being encouraged to try new and challenging activities, by providing activities based on the children's interests.
- Appropriate resources being provided to meet all children's capabilities.

Physical activity in the centre

Physical activity is a planned part of the daily curriculum, including both free play and structured physical activities inside and outside.

The Centre has sufficient indoor and outside play space to allow for a wide variety of physical activities in line with the Physical Activity Guidelines:

- Curriculum planning creates daily opportunities for physical activities.
- Free flow play and sufficient outdoor space encourage physical games and activities, e.g. running, jumping, climbing, riding bikes and scooters, ball games, skipping, hula hoops, bean bags, large block building.
- Movement and play sessions are planned regularly for all age groups, such as tummy crawling, crawling on all fours, rolling, pulling and pushing, climbing, sliding, spinning, dancing.
- Mini-football sessions run by outside coach termly.

Supportive environment

The Centre ensures the environment both inside and outside promotes physical activity by:

(Continued)

(Continued)

- Providing specific equipment, e.g. playground markings, bicycles, climbing frames (large and small, inside and outside), spinners, parachutes etc. Soft room. Planning regular outside trips to parks, playgrounds and city farm.
- Carrying out risk assessments and managing risk through the provision of daily checks of space and environment, written risk assessments, appropriate adult supervision.
- Providing a written procedure for off-site visits.

Involving families

Families are encouraged to take part in physical activity in the Centre both with their children and on their own.

Accurate information is provided to families on national physical activity recommendations through posters, leaflets and parent workshops.

Information regarding keep fit and dancing workshops at the H Pod and other sites in the Euston locality are regularly displayed in the entrance hall.

Active travel

The journey to and from the Centre can provide exercise by way of walking and riding bikes and scooters: it also provides plenty of learning opportunities such as counting, and recognising buildings and roads in the local communities.

The Centre has a travel plan, which is updated annually, encouraging parents to walk or cycle to nursery. Storage for children's scooters is available.

Parents are given road safety packs and staff talk to children about staying safe when walking, cycling or scootering to and from the centre.

Sessions for staff

All staff have attended at least one physical development, including movement-play, training provided by the central training programme, or in-service training. The staff team will review planning and resources for physical activities at least once a year.

Linked policies/guidelines

EYFS
Obesity Targets – Locality target to reduce obesity in children at reception age.

Evaluation and review of the setting's approach to physical activity

We recognise the importance of reflecting on our approach to physical activity. To evaluate our effectiveness we will:

- Consider how other settings approach physical activity
- Include feedback at staff meetings from staff who have attended training
- Review the physical development policy at least once a year in consultation with children and their families
- Obtain feedback from parents, carers and children
- Audit and Review Resources
- Ensure opportunities for physical development are in line with local and national priorities

Date for policy review: November 2015
Signed: Sue Williamson
Date: 24.11.2014

Conclusion

The importance of the policy lies in the impact it has on pedagogy and how practice influences infants' and young children's movement activity.

Higher-quality preschools have been found to implement more moderate to vigorous activity levels than those with lower quality ratings, as measured by ECERS-R (Dowda et al., 2004). High-quality settings provided more opportunities for physical activity, portable and fixed play equipment and, importantly, the practitioners were trained in physical development.

This chapter has attempted to address policy in relation to physical activity in early childhood settings and how that is managed and implemented. Sustaining high-quality practice requires regular monitoring, training and policy updates by effective leaders and managers, all of

Table 6.2 *Physical activity guidelines issued by the chief medical officers of the four countries of the UK (DH, 2011) for children from birth to five years of age*

Age	Length of time	Intensity of activity	Sedentary behaviour	Benefits of movement
Infants, not yet walking	Physical activity should be encouraged from birth, particularly through floor-based play and water-based activities in safe environments.	For infants who are not yet walking, 'physical activity' refers to movement of any intensity and may include the following: • 'tummy time' – this includes any time spent on the stomach, including rolling and playing on the floor • reaching for and grasping objects, pulling, pushing and playing with other people • crawling on all fours, pulling themselves up to standing • 'parent and baby' swim sessions.	Minimising sedentary behaviour is also important for health and development and may include: • reducing time spent in infant carriers, car seats or high chairs • reducing time being restrained in walking aids or baby bouncers • reducing time spent in front of a TV or other screens.	Floor-based and water-based play encourages infants: • to develop their bones and muscles and motor skills, build social and emotional bonds, improves cognitive development and contributes to being a healthy weight.
For children capable of walking	Children of preschool age who are capable of walking unaided should be physically active daily for at least 180 minutes (3 hours), spread throughout the day.	Physical activity is likely to occur mainly through unstructured active play, but may also include more structured activities. Activities can be of any intensity (light or more energetic) and may include: • activities that involve movements of all the major muscle groups – that is, the legs, buttocks, shoulders and arms, plus movement of the trunk from one place to another • energetic play, such as climbing or riding a bike • more energetic bouts of activity, such as running and chasing games • walking/skipping to shops, a friend's home, a park or to and from school.	All under fives should minimise the amount of time spent being sedentary (being restrained or sitting) for extended periods (except when sleeping). Minimising sedentary behaviour may include: • reducing time spent watching TV, using the computer or playing video games • reducing time spent in a pushchair or car seat – this can also help to break up long periods of sedentary behaviour	What are the benefits of being active for at least 180 minutes each day? • Improves cardiovascular health. • Contributes to being a healthy weight. • Improves bone health. • Supports learning of social skills. • Develops movement and coordination.

Individual physical and mental capabilities should be considered when interpreting the guidelines.

which are paramount if the setting is to enhance children's present and future health, well-being, learning and development.

Table 6.2 details the guidelines for all the age groups and you may wish to display it in your setting. Those holding leadership positions could discuss the details with staff, with a view to including these in the setting's physical development policy.

Further reading

Clark, A. and Moss, P. (2011) *Listening to Young Children: The Mosaic Approach* (Second Edition). London: National Children's Bureau.

Department of Health (DH) (2011) 'Start Active, Stay Active: A report on physical activity from the four home countries' Chief Medical Officers' Reference 16306. Available online at: www.gov.uk/government/uploads/system/uploads/attachment_data/file/216370/dh_128210.pdf

Pascal, C. and Bertram, T. (2009) 'Listening to young citizens: The struggle to make real a participatory paradigm in research with young children'. *European Early Childhood Research Journal*, 17 (2): 249–62. Available online at: www.tandfonline.com/doi/full/10.1080/13502930902951486

Siraj, I. and Hallet, E. (2014) *Effective and Caring Leadership in the Early Years*. London: Sage.

Siraj-Blatchford, I. and Manni, L. (2007) 'Effective Leadership in the Early Years Sector: The (ELEYS) study'. London: Institute of Education, University of London.

References

Archer, C.M., and Siraj, I. (2015) 'Measuring the quality of movement-play in early childhood education settings: Linking movement-play and neuroscience', *European Early Childhood Education Research Journal*, 1 (1).

Athey, C. (2007) *Extending Thought in Young Children: A parent-teacher partnership* (Second Edition). London: Paul Chapman.

Barsch, R.H. (1968) *Achieving Perceptual-motor Efficiency: A space-orientated approach to learning* (Vol. 1 of Perceptual-motor curriculum). Seattle, WA: Special Child Publications.

Belsky, J. (2001) 'Emanuel Miller Lecture: Developmental risks (still) associated with early child care', *Journal of Child Psychology and Psychiatry and Allied Disciplines*, 42 (7) 845–59.

Blair, C. and Diamond, A. (2008) 'Biological processes in prevention and intervention: The promotion of self-regulation as a means of preventing early school failure', *Development and Psychopathology*, 20 (3): 899–911.

Blakemore, S.J. and Frith, U. (2005) 'The learning brain: Lessons for education: A précis', *Developmental Science*, 8 (6): 459–65.

Bouffard, M., Watkinson, E.J., Thompson, L.P., Causgrove Dunn, J.L. and Romanow, S.K. (1996) 'A test of the activity deficit hypothesis with children with movement difficulties', *Adapted Physical Activity Quarterly*, 13: 61–73.

British Heart Foundation (2012) 'Factors influencing physical activity in the early years: Fact sheet'. Available online at: www.bhfactive.org.uk/userfiles/Documents/factorsearlyyears.pdf

Brown, W.H., Pfeiffer, K.A., McIver, K.L., Dowda, C.L. and Pate, R.R. (2009) 'Social and environmental factors associated with preschoolers' non-sedentary physical activity', *Child Development*, 80 (1): 45–58.

Bruer, J.T. (2002) 'Avoiding the pediatrician's error: How neuroscientists can help educators (and themselves)', *Nature Neuroscience*, 5 (11): 1031–3.

Burchinal, M.R., Peisner-Feinberg, D.M. and Clifford, R. (2000) 'Children's social and cognitive development and child-care quality: Testing for differential associations related to poverty, gender, or ethnicity', *Applied Developmental Science*, 4 (3): 149–65.

Canning, P.M., Courage, M.L. and Frizzell, L.M. (2004) 'Prevalence of overweight and obesity in a provincial population of Canadian pre-school children', *Canadian Medical Association Journal*, 171 (3): 240–3.

Caroline Walker Trust (2006) 'Eating well for under 5s in childcare'. Available online at: www.cwt.org.uk

Children's Food Trust (formerly School Food Trust) (2012) 'Eat Better, Start Better: Voluntary food and drink guidelines for early years settings in England: A practical guide'. Sheffield: Children's Food Trust. Available online at: www.childrensfoodtrust.org.uk/assets/eat-better-start-better/CFT%20Early%20Years%20Guide_Interactive_Sept%2012.pdf

Clark, A. and Moss, P. (2005) *Spaces to Play: More Listening to young Children Using the Mosaic Approach*. London: Jessica Kingsley Publishers.

Clark, A. and Moss, P. (2011) *Listening to Young Children: The Mosaic Approach* (Second Edition). London: National Children's Bureau.

Coghlan, M., Bergeron, C., White, K., Sharp, C., Morris, M. and Wilson, R.. (2009) 'Narrowing the gap in outcomes for young children through effective practices in the early years'. London: Centre for Excellence and Outcomes in Children and Young People's Services (C4EO). Available online at: http://archive.c4eo.org.uk/themes/earlyyears/ntg/files/c4eo_narrowing_the_gap_full_knowledge_review.pdf

Cosco, N.G., Moore, R.C. and Islam, M.Z. (2010) 'Behavior mapping: A method for linking preschool physical activity and outdoor design', *Medicine & Science in Sports & Exercise*, 42 (3): 513–19.

Cotman, C.W. and Berchtold, N.C. (2007) 'Physical activity and the maintenance of cognition: Learning from animal models', *Alzheimer's & Dementia*, 3 (2 Supplement): S30–S37.

Cotman, C.W., Berchtold, N.C., Christie, L-A. (2007) 'Exercise builds brain health: key roles of growth factor cascades and inflammation', *Trends in Neuroscience*, 30 (9): 464–72.

Daniels, H. (2001) *Vygotsky and Pedagogy*. London: RoutledgeFalmer.

Davies M. (2003) *Movement and Dance in Early Childhood (0–8 years)* (Second Edition). London: Sage.

Department for Education and Department of Health (2011) 'Supporting families in the Foundation Years'. Available online at: www.gov.uk/government/publications/supporting-families-in-the-foundation-years

Department for Education (DfE) (2012) 'Provision for children under five years of age in England: January 2012'. Statistical First Release 13/2012.

Department for Education (DfE) (2014) 'Statutory Framework for the Early Years Foundation Stage (EYFS): Setting the standards for learning, development and care for children from birth to five'. London: Department for Education.

Department of Health (DH) (2011) 'Start Active, Stay Active: A report on physical activity from the four home countries' Chief Medical Officers' Reference 16306. Available online at: www.gov.uk/government/uploads/systems/uploads/attachment_data/file/216370/dh_128210.pdf

Department of Health (DH) (2013) 'Reducing obesity and improving diet'. Available online at: www.gov.uk/government/policies/reducing-obesity-and-improving-diet#issue

Desforges, C. and Abouchaar, A. (2003) *The Impact of Parental Involvement, Parental Support and Family Education on Pupil Achievements and Adjustment: A Literature Review*. Available online at: http://bgfl.org/bgfl/customs/files_uploaded/uploaded_resources/18617/desforges.pdf

Dowda, M., Brown, W.H., McIver, K.L., Pfeiffer, K.A., O'Neill, J.R., Addy, C.L., and Pate R.R. (2009) 'Policies and characteristics of the preschool environment and physical activity of young children', *Paediatrics*, 123 (2): e261–e266.

Dunlop, A.-W. (2008) 'A Literature Review on Leadership in the Early Years'. Learning and Teaching Scotland. Available online at: www.educationscotland.gov.uk/publications/a/leadershipreview.asp

Edwards, A. and Apostolov, A. (2007) 'A cultural–historical interpretation of resilience: The implications for practice', *Critical Social Studies*, 1: 70–84.

Evangelou, M., Sylva, K., Kyriacou, M., Wild, M. and Glenny, G. (2009) 'Early years learning and development: Literature review'. Research Report DCSF-RR176. London: Department for Children, Schools and Families.

Goddard Blythe, S. (2005a) 'Releasing educational potential through movement: A summary of individual studies carried out using the INPP test battery and developmental exercise programme for use in schools with children with special needs', *Child Care in Practice*, 11 (4): 415–32.

Goddard Blythe, S. (2005b) *The Well Balanced Child: Movement and early learning*. (Second Edition). Stroud: Hawthorne Press.

Goddard Blythe, S. (2005c) *Reflexes, Learning and Behaviour: A window into the child's mind: A non-invasive approach to solving learning & behavior problems*. Eugene, OR: Fern Ridge Press.

Goddard Blythe, S., interviewed by Graeme Paton (2014) 'Many children "unable to hold a pencil or sit still" at five', *The Telegraph*, 19 July. Available online at: www.telegraph.co.uk/education/education news/10974849/Many-children-unable-to-hold-a-pencil-or-sit-still-at-five.html

Goswami, U. (2006) 'Neuroscience and education: From research to practice?', *Nature Reviews Neuroscience*, 12 April: 2–7. Online publication, available at: www.uni.edu/gabriele/page4/files/goswami002820060029-neuroscience-and-education.pdf

Greenfield, S. (2001) *The Human Brain: A guided tour* (Reissue). London: Phoenix.

Hands, B.P. and Martin, M. (2003) 'Implementing a fundamental movement skill program in an early childhood setting: The children's perspectives', *Australian Journal of Early Childhood*, 28 (4): 47–52. Available online at: http://researchonline.nd.edu.au/health_article/19

Hannaford, C. (1995) *Smart Moves: Why learning is not all in your head*. Weaverville, NC: Great Ocean Publishers. USA.

Harms, T., Clifford, R. and Cryer, D. (2005) *Early Childhood Environment Rating Scale Revised Edition (ECERS-R)*. New York: Teacher's College Press.

Harms, T., Cryer, D. and Clifford, R. (2006) *Infant/Toddler Environment Rating Scale, Revised Edition (ITERS-R)*. New York: Teacher's College Press.

Heinicke, C.M., Fineman, N.R., Ponce, V.A. and Guthrie, D. (2001) 'Relation-based intervention with at-risk mothers: Outcome in the second year of life', *Infant Mental Health Journal*, 22 (4): 431–62.

Hillman, C.H., Erickson, K.I. and Kramer, A.F. (2008) 'Be smart, exercise your heart: Exercise effects on brain and cognition', *Nature Reviews Neuroscience*, 9 (1): 58–65.

Howard-Jones, P. (2007) 'Transcript of the keynote seminar of the all-party Parliamentary group on scientific research in learning and education: Brain-science in the classroom'. Attlee Suite, Portcullis House, The Institute for the Future of the Mind, 15 May. Available online at: http://susangreenfield.com/assets/Uploads/2007brain-sciencetranscript.pdf

Jensen, E. (2005) *Teaching with the Brain in Mind* (Second Edition). Alexandria, VA: Association for Supervision and Curriculum Development.

Kaplan, C.A. and Owens, J. (2004) 'Parental influences on vulnerability and resilience', in M. Hoghughi and N. Long (eds), *Handbook of Parenting: Theory and research for practice*. London: Sage.

Kranowitz, C.S. (2005) *The Out-of-Sync Child: Recognizing and coping with sensory processing disorder* (Revised). New York: Skylight Press, Perigee Books.

Knowles, G. (2009) *Ensuring Every Child Matters: A critical approach*. London: Sage.

Lamont, B. (2007a) 'Learning and movement'. Available online from the author's website at: http://neurologicalreorganization.org

Lamont, B. (2007b) 'Babies, naturally …'. Available online from the author's website at: http://neurologicalreorganization.org

Lamont, B. (2007c) 'Children who need help'. Available online from the author's website at: http://neurologicalreorganization.org

Lamont, B. (2007d) 'The impact of movement on the mind and its growth'. Available online from the author's website at: http://neurological reorganization.org

Lamont, B. (2009) 'Christopher's Walk'. Unpublished paper.

Lamont, B. (2011) Personal email correspondence with the authors.

Lamont, B. (2014) Personal email correspondence with the authors about a child who had difficulty holding himself in an upright position, whether sitting or standing, and whose body and limbs could best be described as floppy or weak.

Little Steps to Healthy Lives (2013) A programme run by the London Borough of Camden, Children and Young People's Health Improvement Team and Integrated Early Years Service.

London Borough of Camden (2009) *Moving, Learning and Growing: The role of movement in child play and development*. DVD produced by Camden's Integrated Early Years Service.

Macintyre, C. and McVitty, K. (2004) *Movement and Learning in the Early Years: Supporting dyspraxia and other difficulties*. London: Sage.

Mackett, R. (2004) 'Making children's lives more active'. London: Centre for Transport Studies, University College London.

Mackett, R. (2013) 'Children's travel behaviour and its health implications', *Transport Policy: A Journal of the World Conference on Transport Research Society*, Special Issue, 26: 66–72. Paper supplied by the author.

Mackett, R.L. and Paskins, J. (2008) 'Children's physical activity: The contribution of playing and walking', *Children & Society*, 22: 345–57. Paper supplied by the author.

Mathers, S., Linskey, F., Seddon, J. and Sylva, K. (2007) 'Using quality rating scales for professional development: Experiences from the UK', *International Journal of Early Years Education*, 15 (3): 261–74.

Maude, P. (2008) 'How do I do this better?: From movement development into physical literacy', in D. Whitebread and P. Coltman (eds), *Teaching and Learning in the Early Years* (Third Edition). Abingdon: Routledge.

Maude, P. (2010) 'Physical literacy and the young child'. AIESEP Conference Paper.

McCartney, K., Dearing, E., Taylor, B.A. and Bub, K.L. (2007) 'Quality child care supports the achievement of low-income children: Direct and indirect pathways through caregiving and the home environment', *Journal of Applied Developmental Psychology*, 28 (5–6): 411–26.

McPhillips, M. and Sheehy, N. (2004) 'Prevalence of persistent primary reflexes and motor problems in children with reading difficulties', *Dyslexia: An International Journal of Research and Practice*, 10 (4): 316–38.

McPhillips, M., Hepper, P.G. and Mulhern, G. (2000) 'Effects of replicating primary-reflex movements on specific reading difficulties in children: A randomised, double-blind, controlled trial', *The Lancet*, 355: 537–41.

McWilliams, C., Ball, S.C., Benjamin, S.E., Hales, D., Vaughn, A. and Ward, D.S. (2009) 'Best-practice guidelines for physical activity at child care', *Journal of the American Academy of Pediatrics*, 124 (6): 1650–9.

Melhuish, E.C. (2003) 'A literature review of the impact of early years provision on young children, with emphasis given to children from disadvantaged backgrounds'. Institute for the Study of Children, Families & Social Issues, Birkbeck, University of London, prepared for the National Audit Office, London.

Melhuish, E.C., Sylva, K., Sammons, P., Siraj-Blatchford, I., and Taggart, B. (2001) 'The Effective Provision of Pre-school Education (EPPE) Project: Technical paper 7: Social/behavioural and cognitive development at 3-4 years in relation to family background'. London: Institute of Education, University of London and DfEE.

Melhuish, E.C., Sylva, K., Sammons, P., Siraj-Blatchford, I., Taggart, P. and Phan, M. (2008) 'Effects of the home learning environment and preschool centre experience upon literacy and numeracy development in early primary school', *Journal of Social Issues*, 64: 157–88.

O'Callaghan, R.M., Griffin, E.W. and Kelly, Á.M. (2009) 'Long-term treadmill exposure protects against age-related neurodegenerative change in the rat hippocampus', *Hippocampus*, 19 (10): 1019–29. Paper provided by author.

O'Callaghan, R.M., Ohle, R. and Kelly, Á.M. (2007) 'The effects of forced exercise on hippocampal plasticity in the rat: A comparison of LTP, spatial- and non-spatial learning', *Behavioural Brain Research*, 176 (2): 362–6. Paper provided by author.

Office for National Statistics (2012) 'Statistical bulletin: Families and households, 2012'. Available online at: www.ons.gov.uk/ons/dcp171778_284823.pdf

Ofsted (2012/13) 'The report of Her Majesty's Chief Inspector of Education, Children's Services and Skills: Early years'. Available online at: www.ofsted.gov.uk/resources/report-of-her-majestys-chief-inspector-of-education-childrens-services-and-skills-early-years

Pachter, L.M. and Dumont-Mathieu, T. (2004) 'Parenting in culturally divergent settings', in M. Hoghughi, and N. Long (eds), *Handbook of Parenting: Theory and research for practice.* London: Sage.

Panksepp, J. (1998) *Affective Neuroscience: The foundations of human and animal emotions.* New York: Oxford University Press.

Panksepp, J. (2010) 'Science of the brain as a gateway to understanding play: An interview with Jaak Panksepp', *American Journal of Play*, pp. 245–77.

Parents, Early Years Learning (PEAL) project (2006) Joint project between the National Children's Bureau, Coram Family and London Borough of Camden. For more information, visit PEAL's website at: www.peal.org.uk

Parents, Early Years and Learning (PEAL) (2009–2012) 'Making it REAL 2009–12'. Available online at: www.peal.org.uk/real/making-it-real-2009-12.aspx

Pascal, C. and Bertram, T. (2009) 'Listening to young citizens: The struggle to make real a participatory paradigm in research with young children', *European Early Childhood Education Research Journal*, 17 (2): 249–62. Available online at: www.tandfonline.com/doi/full/10.1080/13502930902951486

Peisner-Feinberg, E.S., Burchinal, M.R., Clifford, R.M., Culkin, M.L. Howes, C. Kagan, S.L., Yazejian, N., Byler, P., Rustici, J. and Zelazo, J. (2000) 'The children of the cost, quality, and outcomes study go to school: Technical report'. Chapel Hill, NC: University of North Carolina at Chapel Hill, Frank Porter Graham Child Development Center.

Play England (2011) 'Save Children's Play' flyer and action pack. Available online at: www.playengland.org.uk/resources/save-children's-play-flyer.aspx

Reilly, J.J., Kelly, L., Montgomery, C., Williamson, A., Fisher, A., McColl, J.H., Lo Conte, RL., Paton, J.Y. and Grant, S. (2006) 'Physical activity to prevent obesity in young children: Cluster randomised controlled trial', *British Medical Journal*, 333: 1041.

Roberts-Holmes, G. (2011) Lecture at Institute of Education, Masters in Early Years Childhood Studies: Research Methods, Session 8, Questionnaires and interviews.

Rutter, M. (2006a) *Genes and Behavior: Nature–nurture interplay explained.* Malden, MA: Blackwell.

Rutter, M. (2006b) 'Implications of resilience concepts for scientific understanding', *New York Academy of Sciences*, 1094: 1–12.

Rutter, M., Bishop, D., Pine, D., Scott, S., Stevenson, J., Taylor, E. and Thapar, A. (2010) *Rutter's Child and Adolescent Psychiatry* (Fifth Edition). Oxford: Wiley-Blackwell.

Sacks, O. (2007) *The Man Who Mistook His Wife for a Hat*. London: Picador.

Sigmund, E., Sigmundova, D. and El Ansari, W. (2009) 'Changes in physical activity in pre-schoolers and first-grade children: Longitudinal study in the Czech Republic', *Child: Care, health and development*, 35 (3): 376–82.

Siraj-Blatchford, I. (2004) 'Educational disadvantage in the early years: How do we overcome it? Some lessons from research', *European Early Childhood Education Research Journal*, 12 (2): 5–20.

Siraj-Blatchford, I. (2009) 'Conceptualising progression in the pedagogy of play and sustained shared thinking in early childhood education: A Vygotskian perspective', *Educational and Child Psychology*, 26 (2): 77–89.

Siraj, I. and Hallet, E. (2014) *Effective and Caring Leadership in the Early Years*. London: Sage.

Siraj-Blatchford, I. and Manni, L. (2007) 'Effective Leadership in the Early Years Sector: The (ELEYS) study'. London: Institute of Education, University of London.

Siraj-Blatchford, I., and Siraj-Blatchford, J. (2009) 'Improving children's attainment through a better quality of family-based support for early learning', Early Years Research Review 2. London: Centre for Excellence and Outcomes in Children and Young People's Services (C4EO). Available online at: http://archive.c4eo.org.uk/themes/early years/familybasedsupport/files/c4eo_family_based_support_kr_2.pdf

Siraj-Blatchford, I., Melhuish, E., Taggart, B., Sammons, P. and Sylva, K. (2011) 'Performing against the odds: Developmental trajectories of children in the EPPSE 3–16 study'. Department for Education Research Report DFE-RR128. London: Department for Education

Siraj-Blatchford, I., Sylva, K., Muttock, R., Gilden, R. and Bell, D. (2002) 'Researching Effective Pedagogy in the Early Years' (REPEY). Department for Education and Skills Research Report 356. Norwich: HMSO.

Siraj-Blatchford, J. (2010) 'Surveys and questionnaires: An evaluative case study', in G. MacNaughton, S.A. Rolfe and I. Siraj-Blatchford, *Doing Early Childhood Research: International perspectives on theory and practice* (Second Edition) Maidenhead: Open University Press. pp. 233–8.

Soliday, E. (2004) 'Parenting and children's physical health', in M. Hoghughi and N. Long (eds), *Handbook of Parenting: Theory and research for practice*. London: Sage.

Sunderland, M. (2007) *What Every Parent Needs to Know: The remarkable effects of love, nurture and play on your child's development*. London: Dorling Kindersley.

Sylva, K., Melhuish, E., Sammons, P., Siraj-Blatchford, I. and Taggart, B. (2012) 'Effective Pre-school, Primary and Secondary Education Project (EPPSE 3–14): Influences on students' development from age 11–14'. Research Brief DFE-RB202. London: Department for Education.

Sylva, K., Melhuish, E., Sammons, P., Siraj-Blatchford, I. and Taggart, B., with Hunt, S., Jelicic, H., Barreau., Grabbe, Y., Smees, R., Welcomme, W. (2008) Effective Pre-School and Primary Education 3–11. Final Report from the Primary Phase: Pre-school, School and Influences on Children's Development During Key Stage 2 (Age 7–11) Research Brief DCSF-RB061.

Sylva, K., Melhuish, E., Sammons, P., Siraj-Blatchford, I., Taggart, B. and Elliot, K. (2004) 'The Effective Provision of Pre-school Education (EPPE) Project: Findings from pre-school to end of Key Stage 1'. Institute of Education, University of London, University of Oxford, Birkbeck, University of London, and Sure Start for the Department for Education and Skills. Nottingham: DfES Publications.

Sylva, K., Siraj-Blatchford, I. and Taggart, B. (2006) *Assessing Quality in the Early Years: Early Childhood Environment Rating Scale Extension (ECERS-E): Four curricular subscales*. Stoke-on-Trent: Trentham Books.

The Royal Society (TRS) (2011) 'Brain Waves Module 2: Neuroscience: Implications for education and lifelong learning'. RS Policy document 02/11, DES2105. London: The Royal Society.

Tierney, A.L. and Nelson, C.A. (2009) 'Brain development and the role of experience in the early years', *Zero to Three*. pp. 9–13. Available online at: http://main.zerotothree.org/site/DocServer/30-2_Tierney.pdf

Tremarche, P.V., Robinson, E.M. and Graham, L.B. (2007) 'Physical education and its effect on elementary testing results', *Physical Educator*, 64 (2): 58–64.

Trost, S.G., Ward, D.S. and Senso, M. (2010) 'Effects of child care policy and environment on physical activity', *Medicine and Science in Sports and Exercise*, 42 (3): 520–5.

Tucker, P., van Zandvoort, M.M., Burke, S.M., Irwin J.D. (2011) 'Physical activity at daycare: Childcare providers' perspectives for improvements', *Journal of Early Childhood Research*, 9 (3): 207–19.

Van Praag, H. (2009) 'Exercise and the brain: Something to chew on', *Trends in Neuroscience*, 32 (5): 283–90.

Vygotsky, L.S. (1978) *Mind in Society*. Cambridge, MA: Harvard University Press.

World Health Organization (WHO) (2013) 'Obesity and overweight'. Fact sheet No 311. Online resource available at: www.who.int/mediacentre/factsheets/fs311/en

Index

Page numbers in *italics* followed by *c/f/t* indicate case studies, figures or tables

Miami-Dade College
Homestead Campus Library

500 College Terrace
Homestead, FL 33030-6009